The Robin's Gaze

Book One of Alvin's Journey
J.E. McCarthy

West Front Media, LLC

Copyright © 2024 by J.E. McCarthy and West Front Media, LLC

All rights reserved.

No part of this publication may be reproduced, distributed, or transmitted in any form or by any means, including photocopying, recording, or other electronic or mechanical methods, without the prior written permission of the publisher, except as permitted by U.S. copyright law. For permission requests, contact [include publisher/author contact info].

The story, all names, characters, and incidents portrayed in this production are fictitious. No identification with actual persons (living or deceased), places, buildings, and products is intended or should be inferred.

Book Cover by MiBL Art

First edition 2024

This book is dedicated to all of the readers who have grown to love the McGinn family as much as I have.
J.E. McCarthy

LITTLE ROBIN

I am that little robin,
That sits upon a tree.
I sing to you each morning,
But you don't know it's me.
I am that little robin,
In your garden every day.
I will never leave you,
I will never fly away.

- John F Conner

One

Ireland 1906

Alvin's back ached to his core as he straightened and stretched. He was only twenty-one, but the pounding on his joints from cutting peat turves was taking its toll. His muscles seemed fine. It was his back, knees and ankles that hurt the most. He thought about ways to change things up, so sometimes he cut peat with his right foot driving the shovel and sometimes with the left. The reality was that cutting peat was hard labor no matter how he approached it.

His brother Kellen and father Ambrose were each working their own sections of the bog. He was the fastest on most days and liked to remind Kellen of that fact. He was two years older and in child years, two years is a big head start.

Alvin snuck a look at Kellen's peat footings to get an idea of how far ahead he might be. They cut peat with a long shovel and stood the turves as they were called in a rough pyramid to dry. Ambrose had taught them that there were always four turves to a footing. As he looked at Kellen's work, he nodded with approval. Kellen had two long rows of footings and Alvin realized that there were too many to count. Then he looked at his one long row with pride. *That's a good day's work*, he thought.

He looked at Kellen's rows again and realized that if it were one long row instead of two, Kellen's might be longer. *That can't happen,* he thought and started cutting faster. The late afternoon sun was starting to set, and he felt like he might be able to catch Kellen if he worked fast enough.

Sweat ran from his mop of brown hair stinging his eyes and dripping constantly from the end of his nose. Each drop caused an annoying tickle that made him want to stop to wipe his face. He leaned forward to dig and the sweat just flowed faster.

Alvin snuck another peek and realized that there was no way he'd catch Kellen. He felt a bit foolish being so competitive over digging sod, but there was something about being the oldest that made him want to keep the rivalries in his favor. They were digging the sod for themselves to burn in the winter, so it really wasn't paying anything today. It was far cheaper than coal or wood and it was on their land. Well, the land they worked. The McGinns worked as tenant farmers for Lord Oliver Ellingwood. Ellingwood was the landlord in name only. He hadn't been to his Ireland estate as long as Alvin could remember.

Ellingwood inherited the plantation of more than seven hundred acres from his father, and his father from his father, and so on, all the way back to the 1700's. Alvin had met Lord Ellinwood one summer when illness in England sent many of the wealthy landowners to their estates in Ireland, until the illness ran its course, and it was safe to return.

Lord Ellingwood spent the summer of 1900 in Ireland and Alvin had made some extra money catching salmon from the river to sell at the manor house. Ellingwood had a large entourage with lots of servants. The household bought their food in town, or had it brought from England, but the servants were on their own if they wanted anything that wasn't the mundane fare of the lower house.

On the day he met Lord Ellingwood, he was walking to the manor house with his catch in a creel he and his father had woven from reeds. The groundskeeper, MacNeill, met him near the front gate. Mac Neill was a tall, broad-shouldered Scotsman with a thick mane of curly gray hair. Whenever Alvin saw him without a cap, He has amazed at how tight the curls were. It reminded him of sheep's wool.

At the sight of Alvin, MacNeill grinned and even seemed to lick his lips at the thought of a meal of fresh fish. "Well now. Young McGinn. What have ya today?"

"Salmon. Two good ones. Fresh caught." Alvin opened the cover of the creel to reveal two thick salmon cleaned and ready for the pan.

"Oh my. Those are lovely." MacNeill reached into his pocket and Alvin heard the jingle of coins. "Usual price?"

Alvin grinned and nodded.

MacNeill held a handful of coins in his palm and counted out a few, then add a couple more. "Here you go." He poured the coins into Alvin's hand and pulled the two fish from the creel. He reached back and pulled a newspaper from his back pocket and wrapped the fish in it. "That'll hold em' until I can get them cooked."

Alvin smiled and squeezed the coins in his hand. "Thank you, Mr. MacNeill."

"No, thank you, son. I'll eat like a king tonight," and patted his stomach.

Alvin could hear hoofbeats coming across the field toward them. The Ellinwood's were returning from a hunt and a member of the party was riding toward them at a gallop.

MacNeill could see Alvin about to bolt and reached out to tap his arm. "Easy son. It's Lord Ellingwood's son Richard. He's just trying to make us nervous."

"Why?"

"He's a horse's arse. No more than that, really."

The big chestnut horse was pounding toward them, and Alvin could start to feel the ground tremble under the horse's hoofbeats. It was coming closer, and Alvin could see the lather on its hide. He had been worked hard on the hunt.

Alvin felt the urge to run, then saw the rider smiling with a menacing look of triumph at making them uneasy and he felt the urge to run turn to an urge to fight.

When Ellingwood reached fifteen feet or so he pulled the horse up hard and dirt flew into the faces of Alvin and MacNeill.

Ellingwood yanked the reins and faced them sideways, looking down on them from the great beast. "What's going on here MacNeill? Theft?" Richard Ellingwood was the fattest boy that Alvin had ever seen. He had blond hair, blue eyes and cheeks so fat they could rival most of the pigs in town. Alvin tried to think if he had ever seen a fatter boy but couldn't think of any.

MacNeill frowned. "No M'lord. Just buyin' me supper," opening the paper to show the fish.

"River fish taste like the river. That's where everyone's piss and shit flows into. Enjoy your shit fish."

Ellingwood turned to Alvin. "You. Where did you catch those?"

Alvin paused at the absurdity of the question. "In the river, lord."

Ellingwood grew red in the face. "My lord and I know you caught them in the river. But where on the river? On our land?"

"I don't honestly know."

"Well, you should know. We own the most land, so it likely is ours, and now you are poaching our game and selling it back to us."

A second rider approached. He looked like a much older version of the fat Lord Ellingwood. "Is something amiss?" he asked from a distance.

Richard turned in the saddle. "Poaching is amiss."

Oliver Ellingwood chuckled, "Are you the Sherrif of Nottingham? Protector of the King's Forest?"

Richard stiffened at the comment. "He caught those fish in the river standing on our land. That makes them our fish, and now this *boy* is selling our fish, to our servants."

"Richard. Go to the stable and tend to your horse. Fish are not part of the land. If that were the case, we'd be at odds with half of the village. It's a fishing village. Therefore, the villagers' fish. Can you understand that?"

"But?" protested Richard.

Oliver held up a hand which indicated that the conversation was over, then pointed to the stable.

Richard's face reddened at the dismissal, and he took a breath. "I'm not..."

Lord Ellingwood tapped his heels on the horse's sides and moved forward.

"You will do as you are told without question, or you may return to London and take your chances with whatever plague is running rampant through the streets. Now go."

Richard turned and glared at Alvin and MacNeill then snapped the reins, sending the big stallion galloping for the stables.

Lord Ellingwood turned to the pair. "Please accept my apologies for my son's behavior. He can be a little overzealous at times."

"Think nothing of it M'lord," said MacNeill with a bow of his head.

"Good afternoon, gentlemen." He turned his horse and headed toward the stable as well, then stopped and turned back.

"Oh, MacNeill." MacNeill jumped at the being spoken to again. "Please use the service gate for your purchases. Business at the front gate is unseemly."

"Of course, M'lord. It won't happen again."

"Thank you. Now please return to work. We have guests this evening, and I won't have the grounds looking like some patchwork quilt." Lord Ellingwood turned and rode to the stables at a gallop.

That was the only time Alvin had ever met Lord Oliver Ellingwood. Upon returning to England late that summer, he fell ill and died of an infection before the leaves turned. A land manager was hired, and a few men were kept at the house to maintain the manor, but the Ellinwoods rarely returned to Ireland.

Alvin looked at Kellen's rows again and accepted his defeat. *He'll crow like a young cock*, he thought. *Time to take my medicine*. Ambrose and Kellen had quit for the day and started walking toward him. Kellen was broad shouldered and had a smile as broad as his face would allow. Ambrose looked tired and shook his head slowly with a look of knowing. The student has mastered the teacher.

Alvin tossed his shovel to the ground and pulled a rag from his pocket to wipe his face. "I think you won the day, brother. How did you get two rows so fast?"

Kellen smiled and tapped the side of his head. "I'm smart that's how."

Alvin looked at him and shrugged, "so?..."

Kellen paused and seemed like he might not reveal his secret, but then relented. "I work in both directions."

Alvin frowned, "What the hell is that supposed to mean?"

Ambrose cleared his throat. "He works both right and left-handed. Not just in a straight line. I don't know why it's faster, but I somehow it is."

Alvin caught the meaning of Ambrose's comment. It went against everything they had ever been taught and somehow this kid had figured out a better way. Kellen was becoming his own man.

They gathered up their tools and were about to leave when a girl called out from down the road. "Fresh Fish! Salmon...trout! Caught today!"

The three men turned and looked at the girl. It was Edna Collins. She was a teenaged beauty from town. Her family were fishermen, and she was the seller. Her father Padraig was convinced that people would buy from a girl far more often than a boy.

When Alvin heard that, he remembered thinking that Mr. Collins was probably right. She was a singular beauty with soft brown hair and deep blue eyes. She might have been fifteen, possibly sixteen, and Alvin loved seeing her. She was quiet and seemed a bit shy, and somehow it calmed him to look at her. "What do you have for us?" he called out and Edna smiled.

She brought a wicker basket to him and lifted a cloth from on top of the fish. There was a mix, but one large trout stood out to him.

"How much for that one?" he asked.

Edna looked at the fish and smiled at Alvin. "Sixpence"

"Bah, you should be wearing a mask. That's robbery!" said Kellen.

"Kellen. Mind yourself," said Ambrose. He smiled at Edna and looked to Alvin.

Alvin reached into his pocket and pulled a few coins from his pocket. "Here you go."

Alvin dropped close to a shilling into her hand and took the trout from her basket.

She looked at him, perplexed to have the extra coins.

"The rest is for you," Alvin said with a grin.

She smiled. "Thank you." She tucked the coins into a little pocket in her skirt and covered the fish in the basket with the cloth. "They start to smell if I don't cover em'."

He took his fish by the gills and watched her as she walked away. He turned to his father and brother. "I'm going to marry that girl one day."

Kellen shook his head. "Jaysus, Al, she's a child."

"She'll be a woman one day soon and she'll be my wife. You wait and see."

Ambrose stepped in and took the fish from Alvin. "Okay boys. Let's get this trout to your mother and we'll have a little treat with dinner."

They picked up their tools and started for home. "Wait and see," Alvin said again. "She'll be my wife."

Two

Kellen came running across the bog with a face as red as a beet. He was out of breath and dripping with sweat. He bent over with his hands on his knees, gasping and holding up a finger in a motion to wait. He stood up straight and took a couple of deep breaths.

Ambrose stood, leaning on his shovel. "For the love of God, Nellie. Collect yourself and spit it out."

Alvin chuckled at the comment.

Kellen frowned. "The Ellingwood's are selling the estate. They're selling the manor house to some Protestant Vicker from Belfast and all the land to whoever can afford it."

"A protestant? It'll be a small congregation around here," said Ambrose.

"In town, they said that he's keeping a hundred acres and the house, but he's selling the rest to fund a new church. A protestant church."

Ambrose rolled his eyes. "Well, he wouldn't be building a cathedral now, would he? Of course, it's a protestant church."

"But he's a protestant." Kellen protested.

"Who cares?" said Alvin. "We don't go to church other than Easter and holy days. That hardly makes us good Catholics."

Kellen leaned in. "Yes, but nearly every family in town is Catholic."

Ambrose looked at Kellen. "What's his name? This Vicker?"

"McIlroy, they said."

"So, he's Irish?" asked Ambrose.

Kellen began to relax. "I suppose so."

Ambrose pointed a bony finger at Kellen. "We're Irish first and Catholics and protestants second. Irish need to help Irish."

"Did they say what he's charging per acre?" asked Alvin. "That's what I care about. I don't give a fig about church."

Kellen crossed himself. "For the love of God Al, don't blaspheme."

"It seems to me that every person in this town has prayed and prayed, and they still don't have a pot to piss in. It's not from a lack of working either. We'll only be free when we own the land we work."

Ambrose held up a hand and the squabbling stopped. "Alvin has a good point. How much?"

"They said land on the river is about 12 pounds an acre and the further in land the lower the prices."

"How low?" asked Alvin.

"Grazing land that you can't plant on could be as low as four pounds. They said there are some money lenders in town too if you can't pay cash or get a loan from a bank. They're English from Liverpool."

Ambrose laughed aloud and pulled a clay pipe from his pocket and lit it. He drew a long draw of smoke and let it out slowly.

"What's so funny Da?" asked Kellen.

"Money lenders from England?" He took another puff. "They'll own the whole estate before this is done. Mark my words. Everyone will line up for a loan and they'll hold the notes. When people have a bad crop, or someone gets ill and doesn't pay or just can't do the math, they'll foreclose. Then they'll be the new Lord Ellingwood."

Kellen frowned. "Well, how are we supposed to buy land if we can't get a loan?"

Alvin pushed his shovel into the ground and left it standing by itself. He pulled a cloth from his back pocket and wiped his brow. "Buy what you can afford." He jammed the cloth back in his pocket.

Kellen shook his head. "Together, we can only afford a handful of any decent acres. Maybe only two on the river."

Ambrose tapped his pipe on his heel and put it back in his pocket. "What the hell do you want river frontage for?"

"Fishing. What else," said Kellen.

Alvin laughed. "Yeah, us and everyone else in town. People will buy an acre here and there and triple the number of fishermen on the river. They'll all go broke when they fish the river out. The only ones who make any money fishing, fish the ocean and you'd need a boat for that. Not land."

Ambrose nodded and pointed at Alvin. "Listen to him. He's right. We could pick up a couple of acres for gardening and but a bigger lot for grazing. Sheep are good. Wool, lambs, mutton. You can make a decent living off it."

"Shoveling shit all day. That doesn't sound like much of a living."

Ambrose picked up his shovel. "The borrower is slave to the lender. Never forget it."

Kellen picked up his shovel and started cutting a row of turf. "I've got some money saved. I think I might go my own way Da."

"Suit yourself. I'll never hold you boys back. Make something of yourselves. That would make me happiest."

"What about Ma?" asked Alvin.

"She'll be happy too. As long as one of you starts making some grandbabies along the way. Your brother and sister might have families someday, but that will be a long time, and she wants grandbabies soon."

Kellen laughed and pointed at Alvin. "That'll be him. Him and his fish monger wife."

Alvin snickered. "Don't talk about my future wife that way. Besides, no one will marry you, so I don't think babies are in your future. Oh, wait... Maybe you should pray for a wife. Hahaha!"

"Piss off, you skinny feck. I'll find my wife when I'm ready." Kellen started digging faster.

"That's enough. Dig the lead out of your arses, and get this turf cut. It's going to rain soon, and I don't want to be out here with rain pissin' down on my head, listening to you two bicker about women you never even kissed."

※ ※ ※ ※

At the end of the day, they gathered tools and started for home. Alvin saw Edna with her basket coming up the road.

"I'll catch up later," he said.

Ambrose and Kellen saw Edna. Kellen smiled. "Good luck Romeo."

Alvin gave him a wink. "I don't need luck. I'll pray."

"Piss off." Hissed Kellen with a grin, and he and Ambrose started up the road toward home.

Alvin hurried down the road to meet Edna. As he approached, he could see her face light up and she removed the cloth from the basket to reveal her catch. "I've got some good salmon today," she said with a soft smile.

Alvin blushed a little. "I have no money today."

"Oh." She placed the cloth back over the fish.

"I'm sorry. I'm saving."

She crinkled her brow a little. "Saving for what?"

THE ROBIN'S GAZE

"Land. I'm going to have my own place here someday. Once we find a good spot."

She stopped and looked at him. "You can afford land?"

He straightened and smiled. "Yes. Some. No great estate, but enough for a start. I can't really afford much of a house, but that will come with time."

Edna studied him with her blue eyes and chuckled. "Alvin McGinn, you're the most peculiar lad I've ever met. You are never making comments about getting me out of me knickers. You don't brag about this or that. You're just a good man."

Alvin could feel himself turning red.

"And you blush. You really are a good man."

Alvin was flustered. Completely unmanned by a teenaged girl. "Good enough to marry someday?"

That stole the smile from her face, and she stood in stunned silence. "Usually, boys want to kiss me or... well, you know, something more."

"I want to kiss you, too. But I'd settle for walking with you a bit."

She grinned and nodded, then clutched her basket in front of her. "It's a free road."

They walked and talked for a couple of miles until she had sold her catch. They turned and started back toward town. As they walked, Alvin felt a raindrop hit his cheek. "Damn" he muttered aloud.

"What's wrong?" she asked.

"My Da said it would rain."

Edna grinned. "I like the rain. It makes everything feel cleaner."

"I suppose it does." The rain started falling harder and made puddles on the road.

"I'm worried for you, though."

Alvin stopped quick and shot her a look. "Me?"

"Yes. You're so sweet you might just melt in this rain." Enda stomped in the puddle and got mud on his shoes and pants, then ran ahead laughing hysterically.

He gave chase and when he caught her, he spun her around and kissed her on the mouth. It was only the second time he had ever kissed a girl. The first time was on a dare when the neighbor's cousin came to visit, and although thrilling, he never saw her again. This was different. Her lips were full and soft. He didn't really know what he was doing, but somehow it felt right to him. They kissed for what seemed like a very long time. It was probably only a dozen seconds or so, but it felt long. When they separated, he looked into her eyes and he felt his heartbeat quicken.

"MOOOOO."

They both turned to see a Heffer chewing hay and watching them over a rock wall.

"She seemed to enjoy it," he said. "I hope you did."

Edna squeezed his hand and nodded shyly.

"How old are you?" he asked.

"Thirteen."

THE ROBIN'S GAZE

Alvin's bliss turned to horror, and he pulled away. "Are you serious?"

She paused for a moment and looked a little sad. Then she smiled. "I'm pullin' your leg. I'll be sixteen in September."

"You sneak! You nearly gave me a heart attack. Your father would have skinned me alive."

"Well, you should have thought of that before you seduced me with all your Irish charms."

"I thought we were walking. How's that seducing?"

Edna smiled and took his hand. "Maybe I seduced you. I only walk this way in hopes of seeing you. I could sell my catch faster in town you know."

Alvin was trying to process this new revelation and couldn't think of anything smart to say.

She took his hand. "Let's get walking, or we'll be soaked."

"I'm soaked already," he said with a smile.

They walked along and talked about their dreams. She dreamed of being a mother and he wanted to be a farmer. He liked gardening and tending animals. It felt like the most honest living you could do.

Edna froze in her tracks and pointed. "Stop. Look."

Alvin looked around but didn't see anything out of place. "What? What do you see?" he said with a tension in his voice.

"There's a robin there. I saw it on my way out of town this morning."

Alvin relaxed a bit but wondered if she was about to play a jape upon him. "Is it a special robin?"

"Of course it is. It's my Gram. My Ma's Ma. She died last year and now I see this robin all of the time."

Alvin could see that she believed what she was saying, but he wasn't following the connection. "Are you saying her ghost is in that bird?"

Edna sighed. "Don't be ridiculous. Her soul is in heaven, but your loved ones can see you through the eyes of a robin and that one's been following me, so I know it's her."

"Do you think she saw you kissing me?"

"You kissed me, but why would that matter?"

"Well, I wouldn't want her to tell your Ma, because she'd likely tell Paddy and I'd be bait before I ever get to court you."

"My Gram would want me happy, that's why she's keeping an eye on me...and you. So, mind your manners Mr. McGinn."

They walked along in the soft rain and his eyes were drawn to her wet blouse clinging to her body. He could see her breasts and her nipples seemed to be poking almost through the fabric. He felt excited and tried to keep his mind on more pure thoughts. After all, he wanted her for his wife. But he stole a glance every chance he got.

When they walked to the edge of town, they passed people on the street. A man in his forties walked toward them, grinning like a fiend and licking his lips. His eyes were drawn to her shirt, too. Alvin glared, but the man never noticed him. He was too busy imagining her bare tits in his hands. Alvin could feel the jealousy raging through his veins. He unbuttoned his shirt and took it off, revealing a wet, dingy white undershirt. "Here. I don't want you to get too cold," he said and draped the shirt over her shoulders and blocking the view of her chest entirely.

She pulled the shirt tightly around her. "Thank you. I am a bit cold."

Alvin saw her face change a little when she smelled the shirt. "Sorry it stinks. I've been working all day."

Edna smiled, "It's better than fish." She stopped at the top of a lane of wooden houses that ran along the river. She pulled the shirt off and handed it back to him. "Will I see you tomorrow?"

"You had better believe it."

She looked around and whispered. "I'd like to kiss you again, but someone would tell my father." She slightly puckered her lips and kissed the air, then spun on her heels and scurried down the path to their home.

As she ran away, he stood in the rain grinning like a fool. She might have been the most perfect thing he had ever seen in his life.

Three

Alvin sat on a bench across from St. James's church. He couldn't think of a reason not to go inside but sat there none the less. He had been an altar boy as a child, but as an adult, he lost his appeal for the church. No particular incident, he just questioned in his heart whether the God was real or if it was just a way for ancient people to explain things that they couldn't understand.

He surveyed the empty street and felt a little guilty for not going inside. He considered himself a *holy day* Catholic. That way, in case there was a God, he could stand before St. Peter and tell him that he went to church on the important days with a straight face. It was a way to keep his conscience a little clean.

The morning fog was burning off, and he felt the first ray of sunshine on his face. He closed his eyes and tried to soak it in. It felt good. Ireland was so rainy that every day with sunshine felt like a treasure.

THE ROBIN'S GAZE

His bliss was broken by the loud caw of a hooded crow. It was perched on a limb about twenty feet above his head. He liked the hooded crows. They had black heads and wings, but a white chest and back. His father told them that the bird was native to Ireland. That always made Alvin feel proud.

He reached into his pocket and removed a cloth that was wrapped around a thick slice of soda bread. His mother made the bread with black currants, which were his favorite, and Alvin picked a currant out and ate it, then tore off a chunk of bread and tossed it onto the street where the crow could see it. The bird tilted its head and looked from the bread to Alvin, then back again.

"Not enough?" Alvin said aloud and tore another chunk and tossed it a little further from the first piece.

The crow swooped down and collected the bread, then returned to its previous perch. It snapped at the bread in its beak a couple of times and cawed loudly.

"You're welcome," Alvin said and ate another piece of bread himself.

The bells started to ring at St. James's and the mass was over. As the congregation filed out, he stood and walked a little down the street. He was hoping to catch a glimpse of Edna coming from mass. She and her mother attended every week. Her father and brothers rarely attended because they were busy fishing. He figured they were Holy Day Catholics too.

The throng of parishioners was massive, and soon he felt himself working against the tide of people. He moved onto the grass near the bench to let people by. Alvin stood on his tiptoes and scanned the tops of people's heads, looking for her brown hair. It was more difficult than he had imagined, since most of the women were wearing hats. He could feel himself getting frustrated when he heard his name.

"Alvin McGinn."

He turned and there she was. Brown hair in a bun and her blue eyes were made magical by the sun.

"Good morning, Edna."

She smiled. "Good morning to you, too. Were you looking for something?"

Alvin thought for a moment and grinned. "Salvation?"

Enda laughed out loud and pointed to the church. "Well, salvation lies within. Not across the street."

"If I'm being honest, I arrived late and didn't want to disrupt Father Flynn. If I were to barge in on a service, not on a holy day, he'd think someone needed last rites."

Edna studied him for a moment and whispered. "I know you came to see me. Now you've seen me. What was your plan after that?"

"Walk with me?"

Edna smiled and sighed. "I can't I told my Ma I'd be home directly. She's making dinner for when my father and brothers get home. But you could walk with me as far as the end of the street."

Alvin looked down the street. It couldn't have been more than a couple hundred feet. "Can we walk slow?"

Edna laughed. "A leisurely pace will do."

As they passed the crow, it let out a loud caw and Alvin pulled another chunk of soda bread from his pocket and dropped it on the ground behind him. The bird swooped down and snapped up the bread once again returning to its perch. A few seconds later, it let out a loud caw, and Alvin waved without looking.

"Who are you waving to?" asked Edna.

"Oh, no one. My shoulder is a little stiff that's all. Helps to flail it about a bit."

They walked along, and Alvin tried his best to be charming. Once, when he was a kid, his mother and father took the family to Cork to see his mother's brother before he left for North America. As Cork was near Blarney, Ambrose made a point to bring the family to Blarney Castle. He took Alvin and Kellen to the top and held each one so that they could kiss the Blarney Stone. When they were done Ambrose grinned. "There you go boys, now you have the gift of eloquence."

"What does that mean, Da?" asked Alvin.

"It means the gift of charming speech."

"Have you ever kissed it Da," asked Kellen.

"Oh God no. Local boys piss on it at night."

Alvin and Kellen both wiped their mouths and spat while Ambrose laughed.

Thinking of it made him laugh, because try as he might to find something clever to say, nothing came to mind.

"What's so funny?"

Alvin shook his head. "Just can't believe I'm walking with the prettiest girl in Ireland. I might have to pinch myself to make sure it's not a dream."

Enda stopped and sighed. "Please Alvin, I bet you've said that to every girl you've ever met."

Alvin blushed a little and stopped her. He held her hands and looked into her eyes, then smiled. "It's true. But I never meant it until now."

Edna squeezed his hands and took a long pause. She stared right into his eyes like she was looking at his soul, then leaned in and closed her eyes. She looked as though she was about to kiss him when she opened her eyes and laughed. "My God, Mr. McGinn you think you're a charmer." She released his hands and started walking again.

Alvin stood for a second with his lips still puckered, then realized that he was kissing air. He composed himself and caught up to her. "That wasn't nice to leave me there."

Edna stopped and took his hands. "Mr. McGinn. If you want my heart, it's going to take more than some pretty words."

"Well, I'm going to buy some land," he said as if trying to impress her.

"Lots of men own land and none own my heart."

They walked along until she was at the end of her street. Alvin lifted her hand to his mouth and gently kissed the back of her hand. "I am head over heels for you."

Enda looked at him and smiled. "I know."

She started to turn to walk down her street, and Alvin stood in stunned silence. Enda spun on her heels and kissed him quickly on the cheek. "Me too," she whispered and trotted off to her house.

❀ ❀ ❀ ❀

The next Sunday Alvin sat on the same bench, and the same crow was cawing at him. He didn't really know if it was the same crow, but it was in the same tree.

"Hello, my friend," he said aloud.

The crow tilted its head and cawed. Then, to Alvin's amazement, it looked at the church and flew to the stonework above the door. The crow tilted its head again and cawed loudly.

"Are you inviting me in?" he asked.

The crow cawed again.

"I guess so."

Alvin had been earlier than the previous week, and the last of the parishioners had already entered, but he never saw Edna. He pulled at the handle of the massive wood door and slipped in as quietly as possible. The mass was just beginning, and he tried to make himself as inconspicuous as possible.

Alvin dipped his finger into the font and made the sign of the cross. "In nomine Patris, et Filii, et Spiritus Sancti. Amen," he whispered to himself. He scanned the crowd looking for brown hair in a bun, but it was fruitless. He couldn't see past the hats. It seemed that every woman was wearing a hat, and they all seemed to be white or light blue.

As he was about to give up hope, he saw Edna and her mother sitting up near the front. They were at the end of the pew closest to the wall. *This is my chance*, he thought.

As the processional started, everybody stood. Enda's mother stood on the outside, and Edna was standing next to her. Her father and brothers were not there, so he watched for a moment and decided to make his move. As the processional was climbing the stairs to the altar, Alvin quickly slipped up the outer aisle and stopped next to Edna's mother.

"Pardon me missus, may I?"

Edna's mother smiled and nodded then moved over a little. Edna's eyes were as big as saucers, and she tilted her head in a look of exasperation.

Alvin looked at her mother and smiled. "Thank you, M'am" he whispered, then leaned back, and looked at Edna. She looked near panicked, and he gave her a smile and a wink. Soon she relaxed and shook her head, then focused on the altar.

Every so often, he noticed her looking over at him, so he made a point to appear deep in prayer. He was doing it for her mother's benefit, but when she was able to catch his eye, he made sure to look at her in a way to say he loved her. Something more than youthful lust. When he looked at her, he could see something happening and she looked happy.

After mass, he stepped aside to let her mother pass and her as well. The third person was an elderly man, named Murphy, and he let him pass too before entering his place in line. As soon as Murphy stopped to talk to another parishioner, Alvin slipped by and was right behind Edna and her mother.

When they stepped outside, Alvin smiled and squinted in the sun. "Pardon me Mrs. Collins, may I escort you and your lovely daughter home?"

Ellen Collins was a tough looking red head with short, cropped hair and a face that had been battered by the sun. She was still attractive, but her wrinkles cut deep into her face. She studied Alvin. "You're the McGinn boy, right?"

Alvin squeezed his hat and bowed slightly. "Yes M'am, yes I am."

Ellen smiled and motioned to Edna. "I have already heard enough about you. So, show me that you are the gentleman, she says you are."

Alvin stepped up and offered his elbow. Edna took it and squeezed him gently. As they walked, he thought. *I have never been prouder than at this moment.*

She may not have been the prettiest girl in Ireland, but she was to him. He loved every bit of her. Her sparkling eyes, her beautiful smile, and her laugh. That was the part that he loved the most. To hear her laugh was like heaven to his ears.

When they arrived at the street where she lived, Ellen looked at them both. "I'm going in now. It was a pleasure to meet you, Alvin."

Alvin bowed a little. "You too Mrs. Collins."

Ellen laughed. "Edna, be quick about it. I can't tolerate your father's guff today."

Ellen turned and walked toward their home. Alvin thought, *she moves like a queen.*

Edna smiled and took Alvin by both hands. "Thank you," she whispered and kissed him on the cheek. She squeezed his hands and rushed off next to her mother.

Alvin watched the two women walking away when Edna slipped her hand behind her back and made her fingers into the shape of an L, then as quick as it appeared, it was gone.

L thought Alvin. Then it came to him. *Love.*

Four

Alvin paced from one side of the dock to the other. He had fished plenty, but he wasn't really particularly comfortable on boats. The few times he had been on the river, the constant motion made him queasy. His legs were made for solid ground, not the high seas.

He watched the boat traffic coming up and down the river. The docks were busy with men bringing in their catch and buyers eager to get some fresh fish to market. As he scanned the crafts floating along, he spotted the Ellen Marie. It was Padraig Collins' boat. Everyone knew him as Paddy, and he stood at the bow ready to fend off at the dock. Behind him sat his sons Sean and Finn who manned the oars. It was a medium sized boat with a single mast, that he had heard people call a Hooker before although he didn't really know what that meant. The name was painted on in a very elegant script and was the best-looking part of the boat. Alvin thought to himself and grinned, *I guess if you are going to name a boat after your wife, you'd better make sure at least the name looks good.*

As they pulled into the dock, Paddy caught Alvin's eye and his face became somewhat unfriendly. Alvin suddenly found it hard to swallow, and he felt his heartbeat quicken. *This is lunacy*, he thought. *I should come another day*. He was about to bolt and suddenly, in his mind's eye, he saw Edna smiling at him. It comforted him and took a deep breath, then stepped onto the dock.

Paddy never dropped his gaze from Alvin. He started speaking to his sons without looking at them. "Boy's, get the boat stored and get that catch up as quick as you can. I don't want to be here all afternoon." When he was close enough, he hopped from the boat to the dock and walked toward Alvin.

Alvin's heart jumped again, and he could feel his heartbeat in his throat.

As Paddy approached, his gaze became something between a scowl and a death stare. "You must be McGinn."

Alvin reached a hand out to shake his hand and Paddy looked at the hand for a moment before shaking it. "Yes sir, Mr. Collins. Alvin McGinn."

"So, you want to court my daughter?" Collin said as he eyed Alvin from head to toe.

"Yes sir. I would like your permission if you would see fit."

Collins locked his gaze again. "I heard you already kissed her from some local folks. Why didn't you ask me before that?"

Alvin could feel himself blushing. "Well sir, to be honest that happened all of a sudden, so I didn't have time to think it through."

Collins pulled a clay pipe from his pocket and studied Alvin as he lit it. Collins was a thin man with dark hair and the same deep blue eyes as Edna. He took a long draw and blew the smoke into the air. "Are you planning on becoming a fisherman McGinn?"

Alvin was surprised by the question, but soon composed himself. "No sir, I'm a farmer."

"A farmer?" chuckled Collins. "What kind of farmer?"

Alvin had thought about this question plenty ever since they heard about the breaking up of the Ellingwood estate. "Well, sir. I am planning on buying several acres for a small sheep farm and I'll try to add to it as the farm becomes profitable. The parcel I have in mind isn't much good for any other kind of farming."

Collins smiled. "Good. We have enough fishermen in this village already."

"So, may I court your daughter?"

"Oh, hell no son. Why would she want a dirt farmer when there are a hundred fishermen right here? Look around." He cast his hand across the multitude of men around the docks.

Alvin looked around and saw men of all ages moving about, pulling catches from boats, or bringing the catch to the market. Then he looked Collins straight in the eye. "Because these men will never treat her better than I will. I'm sure plenty of these fellas make more money than I do, but they could never love her as deeply as I do."

"Love?" chuckled Collins. "Christ, son, get ahold of yourself. How can you say you love her?"

Alvin didn't care for being mocked and he stiffened his resolve. "Yes sir, love. I loved her the first moment I laid eyes on her. I bought fish every day that I had any money, just to talk to her and I believe that she is the most beautiful thing that I have ever seen on this earth."

Collins pulled the pipe from his mouth and picked some bits of tobacco from his tongue and looked Alvin in the eye. "Are you a drinker, McGinn?"

Alvin smiled. "No sir. I have had a drop here and there, but to be honest, I save a lot of my money and I spent all my drinking money on fresh fish."

That made Collins laugh aloud. "That's the best money you ever spent. Alright, you can court my daughter. But don't have knowledge of her before you're married. I know all the deep holes in that river, and you'll be sleeping in one if you ever hurt her. Understand?"

"Yes sir, Mr. Collins." Alvin reached out and grabbed his hand, shaking it with a firm grasp.

Alvin spun on his heels and started up the street. His face was one broad toothy smile, and he nodded and greeted everyone that he passed. In the distance, he could see Edna coming toward him with her basket for the day's catch.

He bounded to her and stood before her like a grinning fool. "Your father says I may court you."

Edna's smile vanished. "But what about what I want? What if I didn't want to court you?" she sighed.

Alvin stood speechless and really didn't know what to do. He could feel the heat in his face as he started blushing again. "I guess I must have misunderstood," he said in something above a whisper. He hung his head like a sad dog and started to walk past her.

"I was hoping you'd ask him to marry me," she said with a sly grin.

Alvin shook his head and grabbed her with both arms, twirling her round and round. He placed her on the ground and kissed her. "You're a mean one, you are."

Edna laughed. "I just wanted to see you squirm a bit."

"Well, he's right at the bottom of the hill and seems in a good mood. I'll go ask." Alvin took a couple of long strides back toward the docks when he heard her call out.

"Okay, well played, sir! Best not push your luck."

Alvin stopped and turned back toward her. "I would have asked you know."

Edna stopped and admired him for a moment. He was smart and handsome, and he may have been the most confident man she has ever met for being so young. "I know you would have. That's why I love you."

Alvin smiled and held her hand. "I love you too. Will I see you later? I have to get back to the bog to cut peat."

Edna squeezed his hand. "I suspect I'll make it up there on my journeys."

"I look forward to a discount on fish then, seeing as I'm practically family."

"Huh, my father is *not* a generous a man."

As Alvin walked his way back toward the bog, he passed a line of men in front of a small storefront. The sign above the door said, Wilkes and Booth Financial Services, Liverpool. His father's words came back to him, *the new lords Ellingwood*. As he passed the line, it struck him how many looked nervous, like expecting fathers. Perhaps in some ways they were. Their hopes and dreams were reliant upon the quality of the land they were looking to buy and the whims of a foreign banker.

He was about to cross the street when an ornate carriage pulled up and stopped a few feet in front of him. The door flew open, and an enormously fat man stepped out onto the street. It was Richard Ellingwood and his gluttony had become something shocking. His face was red, and he seemed to gasp a little with each breath.

Alvin found himself face to face with him and Ellingwood looked at Alvin as if they knew each other.

"Lord Ellingwood, are you okay?"

Ellingwood teetered a little and Alvin thought that he might be drunk. "That coach is stifling."

Alvin looked at the coach and the windows were opened, but maybe it was the lack of a breeze that was making him so hot. He certainly didn't look well.

Alvin nodded his head "Well good day, M'Lord." As he started by Ellingwood grabbed him hard by his arm. At first, Alvin thought he was trying to hurt him intentionally, but when he looked at Ellingwood's face, he saw terror in his eyes and he was simply trying to remain upright.

Alvin grabbed him by both arms and swung him around so that he was seated on the floor of the carriage rather than letting him fall to the ground. Most of the people in the street knew the lord by sight and they stood gawking. "Someone fetch this man some water. Lots of it."

His driver jumped down from the seat and secured the horses.

Alvin had been near exhaustion from heat enough times to recognize the signs. He helped Ellingwood off with his coat and unbuttoned his shirt. A moment later a woman from the Public House arrived with a pitcher of water. Alvin took it and handed it to Ellingwood. "Just some sips or you're like to get the cramps."

Ellingwood took a few gulps, and Alvin pulled the pitcher away. "Forgive me, Lord." He poured part of the pitcher over Ellingwood's head and down the back of his shirt. Ellingwood took a deep breath and clutched at Alvin's arm again.

"Christ, that's cold!" he said.

"That's good. We need to cool you down."

Ellingwood nodded in understanding. "Where do I know you from?"

Alvin was wetting a handkerchief to cool Ellingwood's face. "I sold some fish at the manor house to Mr. MacNeill. Maybe that's where you remember me from."

"Oh, the fish poacher! Now I remember."

Alvin nodded. "Yes, but I didn't think I was poaching at the time."

"Of course, you weren't. I'm not sure what came over me. Youth perhaps."

Alvin found that funny, since Richard Ellingwood was only a couple years older than him. *Maybe it was because nobles lived a much different life than regular people*, he thought.

Ellingwood's breathing seemed easier and he looked a little less flushed. "Are you feeling better M'Lord?"

Ellingwood motioned for the pitcher again and took a deep swallow. He handed it back to Alvin and wiped his mouth. "I am. I thank you sincerely." He motioned to the driver and reached out toward him. "Smith. Give me a hand up." Together Alvin and Smith helped him to his feet.

Alvin smiled. "I'm glad you're feeling better."

Ellingwood took a deep breath and looked around. By now, the onlookers had moved on. He looked at the line of men in the moneylender's line. "Busy place. Are you buying any of the estate?"

Alvin nodded. "Yes, just what I can afford. Some acres for a small farm and maybe some sheep."

"Why don't you get a loan? The rates are very reasonable."

"My father says the borrower is slave to the lender. And I enjoy my freedom."

Richard laughed aloud. "You are a smart man...I don't know your name."

"Alvin McGinn M'Lord."

Richard reached out and shook his hand. "A pleasure to meet you McGinn."

"Thank you M'Lord. If you are alright, I need to get to work at the peat bog, or my father might think that I have deserted him."

"Of course. I would never keep a man from his labors. And again, I thank you sincerely."

Alvin nodded and started toward the bog at a something close to a run.

Five

It was a damp, foggy morning, like most mornings in the river valley. He walked toward the peat bog with his shovel on his shoulder and a clay pipe in his mouth. He left before his father and brother to get a jump on work in case he could finish in time to see Edna later in the day.

While he walked, he thought about a story he had read once, about a sailor who had traveled the world and visited tropical islands so hot, that the natives hardly wore any clothes at all. *It certainly wasn't this island*, he thought. He loved Ireland, the people, the greenness of the land and of course a pint of Guinness. The one part he did not love entirely was the weather. There were weeks in the summer where the rain was so heavy for so long, that they might have needed a boat to cut peat. It had rained during the night and his shoes had already soaked through. He hated starting a day with wet feet, by the time the day was over, it felt like his skin might come off with his stockings.

As he made the turn to the bog, he heard the sound of hoofbeats coming closer. He moved to the edge of the road so that the riders might not run him down in the fog. He could definitely hear two horses. *Perhaps a carriage*, he thought. But he didn't hear any wheels. The sound was getting louder, and he moved off the road completely to let the riders pass. When they cleared the fog, he could see two men dressed in long frock coats and top hats. They slowed at the sight of him.

One man was clean shaven with fair skinned with pale blue eyes. The other had a thick black mustache and eyebrows with dark eyes that looked nearly black. The man with the mustache studied Alvin carefully. "Are you McGinn?"

Alvin jumped a little at the question. "I am. How do you know that?"

The man with the blues eye produced a paper from his pocket. "We had a description."

Alvin wasn't sure what was happening, but he slid the shovel from his shoulder and gripped it in the event of a fight.

"Easy lad. We mean you know harm," said the man with blue eyes. "I'm Nathaniel Wilkes and this is my partner, James Booth. We have a shop in the village, as you may have noticed the lines."

Alvin relaxed and let the head of the shovel fall to the ground. "I have. But what do you want with me? I don't want a loan."

Booth laughed. "We know. You don't want to be a slave to the lender."

Alvin looked at them carefully. He didn't recall either of them being there when he was helping Lord Ellingwood.

Wilkes dismounted and walked toward Alvin with a folded packet. "We have something for you," he said and handed the packet to Alvin. "Can you read?"

Alvin frowned. "Of course I can read. A man needs to feed his mind and his body."

Wilkes held up a hand. "I meant no offense, sir. Most of the men in the village can't read and most can't write their names."

Booth chuckled from a top his horse. "They can read *Public House* well enough."

That made Alvin laugh. "I'm not so sure they can read it, but they certainly know where it is."

Alvin looked at the parcel. It had a wax seal and an impression of two rampant lions facing each other like a mirror. It was the Ellingwood coat of arms.

"I'll save you the suspense, Mr. McGinn," said Wilkes. "His lordship has gifted you forty acres of grazing land suitable for sheep and other farming."

"Why?"

"Because you helped him yesterday," added Booth.

"I would have done the same for anyone."

Wilkes patted Alvin on the shoulder. "He knows that, but he wanted to give it to you. He appreciates you."

"I don't know what to say. My mind's a mess all of a sudden."

"You are free to do with it what you wish. If you choose to sell it, you can have the money." Said Wilkes.

"Why would I sell it? It was a gift from his lordship."

"Well, you could start a life in the village."

"Or America," called Booth. "Eighty pounds would take you a long way in America. Why you'd practically be nobility with that kind of money over there."

Alvin looked at Wilkes. He was quiet and passive. When he studied Booth, he saw something he didn't like. Booth had the presence of a charlatan. Something akin to a gypsy and a gnawing in his gut told him to be weary.

"I thought that they were getting four pounds an acre for farmland?" asked Alvin.

"They are. But we would need to resell it and of course we would need to maintain a small margin for our services. It's how we stay in business."

Alvin gave them both a look of disbelief. "Fifty percent seems a bit more than a small margin."

Wilkes sighed. "A reader and a mathematician. You're a prodigy in this river valley."

Booth shifted in his saddle. "One hundred pounds. Now that's more than fair McGinn."

"It was a gift. I would never insult his lordship by selling it."

Wilkes extended a hand, and Alvin took it. "I respect your sense of honor. But think on it all the same. Like my colleague said, they say that America is the land of opportunity."

"I love Ireland, and I want to have a family here."

Wilkes smiled. "That should get you off to a strong start. You know where to find us if you change your mind."

Alvin turned to Booth, high up on his horse. "I do. I'll look for the line of slaves," he said with a wink, and tucked the packet into his pocket.

Booth chuckled a little. "Smart Arse."

Wilkes remounted and touched his hat. Then the two men headed back into the fog.

When they were out of sight, Alvin opened the seal and began reading. He smiled and thought, *I'm asking Paddy if I can marry her.* He put the paper back in his pocket. *But maybe I'll wait a bit. He's like to say no if I'm too eager.* He started back toward home to place the documents somewhere safe and as he walked, he thought some more. *To hell with it, I'm asking him.*

❀ ❀ ❀ ❀

Alvin ran to the small house he shared with his parents, Kellen and his two siblings Jameson and Emily. He flung the door open, out of breath and bent forward to steady his breathing.

Kellen shook his head. "That was fast, too much for you today?"

Alvin stood up and plopped the parcel on the table. "I've had a hell of a mornin' so far."

Alvin's mother, Annie, was a slender woman with light brown hair and blue eyes. She eyed the packet and touched the wax seal. "That's Lord Ellingwood's sigil."

Alvin smiled. "It is. He has given me forty acres of farmland as a gift. Can you believe that?"

Ambrose opened the packet and did his best to read the contents. "What in God's name would possess him to do that?"

"I helped him yesterday. That's it."

Kellen frowned. "You helped him, and he gave you forty acres? There must be some other scheme behind it."

Alvin shrugged. "I don't think so," Alvin produced a folded note from his pocket, "and he's invited me to the manor house for dinner."

Annie took the note. "The manor house? My god, son, did you save his life or something?"

"I don't think so. He was just overheated."

"It says you can bring a guest."

"Oh, take me," asked Kellen like some desperate child waiting to be selected for team.

"I'm taking Edna."

The wind left Kellen's body, and his shoulders slumped. "The fish mongers' daughter?"

"My future wife."

"Oh Jaysus, not that again."

Ambrose had been studying the papers. "Kellen. Hush yourself." He stacked the papers neatly. "This all looks official, son. I know the parcel listed here. It has a stream and a small pond. A bit rocky in spots, but plenty of quality acreage for gardens and animals. There's a small cottage as well. But I don't think it's been occupied for twenty years. The roof is thatch, so it's probably rotted by now."

"Roofs can be mended. Is it a good spot to start a family?" asked Alvin.

Ambrose smiled and handed him the stack of papers. "A perfect spot."

Annie reached out and took Alvin's hand. "Get me some grandchildren. You lot are too big to cuddle."

Alvin chuckled. "I'll do me best Ma." Alvin put the invitation back in his pocket. "I need to see about a date for dinner."

Alvin ran to the docks to try to catch Edna before she left to sell the catch. He scanned the crowd of people, trying to get a glimpse of her when he heard his name.

"Well McGinn. Early day? You won't make much money skylarking here."

Alvin turned to see Paddy Collins standing with his arms crossed and a pipe hanging from his lip.

"Yes, sir, I'll have to work faster tomorrow. But I'm looking for Edna."

"She's about here somewhere. But she'll be leaving with the catch soon."

Alvin took a deep breath and exhaled. "Could I have a word in private with you?"

Paddy pulled the pipe from his mouth and studied Alvin for a moment and then gave a jerk of his head to indicate an empty shop stall.

Alvin related the story of helping Lord Ellingwood, the gift of the land, and his plan to start a family. When he got to the part where he explained that he wanted to start that family with Edna. Paddy spat on the ground.

Alvin could see Collins turning the question in his mind. Paddy stared directly into Alvin's eyes without blinking. Alvin felt the weight of the stare pressing down on him, and he somehow felt smaller. *Stand your ground McGinn*, he thought to himself.

Paddy took a puff from his pipe and blew the smoke off to the side. "Start your farm. When you have a suitable place to live. You can marry my daughter."

Alvin thrust his hand out to shake with Collins. "Thank you, sir!"

When Collins shook his hand, he pulled him closer and spoke in something a little above a whisper. "Don't defile her before your wedding night. She's to be treasured. Do you understand me?"

Alvin pulled back a little and nodded. "Mr. Collins. I treasure her above all things on this earth."

Collins released his grip and nodded his approval. "Good lad. When will you ask her?"

"I really hadn't thought about that. Suppose I could just come out with it, but that doesn't seem very romantic."

Collins grinned. "My god, son, you know nothing of women, do you?"

Alvin looked a little deflated. "I don't. They are a mystery to me."

"Ha! You know more than you think. They are a mystery to be sure. But a good woman makes you a better man. I'd be a mess without my Ellen."

"My father says the same about Ma."

Collins placed a hand on Alvin's shoulder. "Find a quiet place, when it's just the two of you and I'm sure it will be fine."

"Thank you, Mr. Collins."

"If you're to marry my Edna, you can call me Paddy."

"Thank you, Paddy."

Collins smiled and patted him on the back then extended his pipe like a pointer. "I see your future coming McGinn. Make it a good one."

Alvin followed the pipe and saw Edna walking up the lane with her basket. He smiled at Paddy and started toward Edna with great strides, trying not to appear too desperate by running. Every time he saw her, he felt she was the most beautiful thing he had ever seen in his entire life.

Six

Alvin watched Edna from across the street. She was magnificent. Her mother helped her put together an ensemble of clothing from friends and family. Her dress was as blue as a sapphire, and she wore long white gloves, which made her look quite elegant. What he was most drawn to, was her hair. It had been put up in a tight bun and it showed her long, slender neck. He was imagining himself kissing her neck when he heard the sound of a carriage driver calling out. "Make way there. Step aside."

The streets were bustling with activity and the carriage was having difficulty making its way through the throng of people. No one on their lane had ever dined at the manor house, and now most of the women were out to see Edna and Alvin. He had kept the gift of land to himself, but as soon as Edna told her mother and aunt about the dinner invitation, the whole lane knew within a day.

Alvin wanted to be there before the carriage and stepped into the street and walked with something akin to a swagger. Stand tall lad, he thought to himself. Like Edna, he borrowed from his father and brother to come up with a suit worthy of dinner with a lord.

When Edna saw him, she smiled and gripped her mother's wrist. She whispered something to her mother and the rest of the ladies seemed to agree and they all smiled at him. That made Alvin blush a little.

Paddy stepped through the crowd of women and smiled. "Well McGinn. Is that yourself? You look a right proper country gent."

Alvin tilted his head and touched the brim of his hat. He was wearing a black suit that was typically reserved for funerals. The hat had belonged to Ambrose's father along with a green and gold waistcoat. All in all, he felt that he appeared quite dapper.

"Thank you, Paddy. I aim to make a good impression."

As he approached Edna, he felt as though he were gliding across the cobblestones, until he at last he lifted her right hand and kissed the back of it. He glanced around to acknowledge the women there and his eyes met with looks of approval. He struggled to think of something clever to say, but he was rescued by the arrival of the carriage from the manor house. The two-person chaise was pulled by a single horse and driver. The driver brought the carriage to a halt in front of the couple. He locked the brake and hopped down as nimble as a cat and opened the half door.

"You first miss." He said with a hand extended to help her up the step. When Edna was seated, he turned to Alvin. "Mind your step, sir."

Alvin jumped in and the driver closed the door behind him. Then, in a single quick movement, the driver was back in his seat and the carriage was rolling. People stared as they rode by, and Alvin began to feel a little self-conscious. He leaned in and whispered in her ear. "They have never seen anything so beautiful as you. That's why they're staring."

Edna made a little fist and knocked him on the leg. "Stop being foolish." She whispered back.

As they cleared the village, the road was flanked by stone walls and fields making for a very pleasant ride.

"Pardon me, driver."

The driver was a smallish man in his fifties with a tightly cropped head of thinning gray hair. "Yes?"

"First, what is your name? I don't want to call you by your job. If that were the case, people would call me *digger*."

"Smith, sir."

"Hello Smith. Do you know how many people will be dining tonight?"

"I suspect just five. His lordship, his wife, her sister and you two."

"Oh. Thank you. I had heard that these dinners were heavily attended. I was nervous to meet so many powerful people."

"Huh," Smith chuckled. "We haven't held those types of gatherings since lord Oliver passed. His lordship doesn't entertain as well as his father did. But that is the challenge of youth. Lord Richard has not been to Ireland enough to make many friends and his friends in London prefer to stay in England. Don't be nervous, son. His lordship is a good conversationalist, and you won't go away hungry. There is always too much food by half."

"Thank you." Alvin leaned back and took Edna by the hand.

"Might I add that you look lovely young lady. I would keep her close if I were you, sir. Don't want her to slip away."

Alvin squeezed her hand and looked at her perfect profile. "Thank you, Smith. I'll hold on tight."

As the carriage entered the gate, Alvin could see a footman standing at attention outside of the front door. The whole situation seemed like a dream to him. The last time he had seen Richard on this property, he was accused of poaching and now he was an invited guest. The carriage slowed and came to a stop. The footman was a black man who appeared to be in his early twenties. Alvin had never seen a black man to talk to. He wondered if he could speak English or if he spoke some form of African.

As he opened the door, he placed a step on the ground and extended a hand to allow Edna to exit gracefully. "Be careful miss," was all he said in perfect English.

Well, that answers that question thought Alvin.

"And watch your step, sir."

THE ROBIN'S GAZE

Edna turned and watched the footman for a moment. She had never seen a black person before, either. "Where are you from?" she asked softly.

"Portsmouth, miss."

"Oh, I mean originally," she said.

"Ah. I see. I was born in Portsmouth, but my parents came to England from Liberia."

"Were they freed slaves from America?" asked Alvin.

Edna gasped. "Alvin. How could you ask such a thing?"

The footman laughed. "No. It is fine miss. My grandparents were freed slaves."

"What is your name?" asked Alvin.

The footman grinned. "My name is White. You can see the humor of the former masters."

Smith cleared his throat. "Your name will be *out of work* if you don't get them inside. His lordship doesn't like to be kept waiting."

"Mr. Smith is correct. This way, please." White led them up the steps and opened one side of the massive white doors.

They entered a grand foyer with a massive staircase that ran along the perimeter of the room.

Alvin and Edna were looking at the paintings in awe when they heard a bellow from above.

"Welcome friends. White, please seat our guests in the salon and I'll be down directly."

White led them into a room with couches facing each other and a fireplace at one end. It was too warm for a fire, so it was covered with a decorative panel. It was the most opulent room either of them had ever seen. The walls had numerous bookcases each completely full of books.

"It would take a lifetime to read all of these books," remarked Alvin.

Edna chuckled. "Well, that would be two lifetimes for me. I can read, but it is a very slow process, and I don't know what a lot of the words mean, so I attempt to look them up in a dictionary."

White walked to a buffet and returned with two crystal glasses. "May I interest you in champagne? They make it at his lordship's family's estate in France."

"Yes, certainly," said Alvin, taking a glass. "Edna?"

She looked at the glass and took it slowly. "Thank you. Mr. White."

White made a short bow and went back to his post beside the buffet.

"I have never had champagne. What if I don't like it?"

"Then just sip it. I'm sure they have something else."

Edna brought the glass to her lips and was startled a little by the tickling of the bubbles. "Don't stare at me." She whispered.

Alvin turned away and took a sip himself. He peeked at her out of the corner of his eye as she drank.

"Very nice. It's so light," she whispered.

Alvin liked it too.

"Mr. McGinn. How nice of you to join us." Alvin looked up to see Lord Ellingwood in the doorway with a woman on each

THE ROBIN'S GAZE

side. They were enough alike that everyone would recognize them as sisters. Both had dark hair and dark eyes. One was taller with a larger mouth, and the shorter one had more of a girlish figure than womanly.

"Allow me to introduce my wife, Eliza-Mae and her sister Laura Harp. I call them my harpies." He laughed so hard that his enormous stomach continued to jiggle for a moment. Neither woman found him funny. "Ladies, this is Alvin McGinn. The man who saved my life a few days ago."

Eliza-Mae made a small nod. "We thank you most profoundly, Mr. McGinn."

"Oh, yes," added Laura.

Alvin was shocked by the statement. "You're welcome, Ma'am. I don't know that his lordship was in any grave danger..."

"Nonsense, you are too modest by far," interrupted Richard. "Please McGinn. Introduce this marvelous creature here with you. Isn't she a beauty ladies?"

"Stunning," said Eliza-Mae, with something of a forced smile.

"Like the sun," added Laura, with no smile at all.

Alvin turned to Edna. "This is my most treasured friend, Miss Edna Collins."

Richard lumbered forward and took her tiny hand in his great swollen palms and kissed the back of her hand. "An absolute pleasure to meet you, Miss Collins."

Edna curtsied and raised her head with a smile. "Thank you for having us M'Lord."

"The pleasure is ours; I assure you." Ellingwood looked around and found the footman. "White, please tell the kitchen I am ready to dine." He motioned a big beefy hand to a set of double doors that lead to a dining room that could easily seat twenty people. "We'll be at the far end."

Alvin had never seen a true dinner in a house like this, but he could imagine it. The numerous guests, a dozen servants or more. It was life that he had only read about in books. The dinner was excellent and there was more food than his family might have eaten in a week.

After dinner, the ladies returned to the salon with Edna in tow and Richard brought Alvin across the hall to his office.

When they sat down, Ellingwood picked up a small bell and rang it. A moment later White was in the doorway awaiting instructions.

"Two cognacs please."

White walked to a cabinet and pulled a crystal decanter from the shelf and poured the liquor into short wide glasses. He brought them on a tray and when each man had his drink, White left and closed the door behind him.

"Please, in this room, or when we are alone, call me Richard. I get tired of the titles. I just want to talk like friends."

Alvin was about to say *yes M'Lord* but nodded and smiled. "Thank you, Richard."

Ellingwood sipped at his cognac. "I suppose you are curious about the land."

"I was completely surprised, to be sure."

"Wilkes said that you refused to sell it. You could have you know. It's a gift to dispose of as you wish."

Alvin smiled. "I know. But I want to have a family here. In Ireland. That land is the key to starting my family."

"With Miss Collins?"

"I haven't asked her yet, but I have her father's blessing."

"What are you waiting for?"

Alvin shrugged. "A romantic time and place, I guess."

"Smart man. My marriage was arranged by my father and Lord Harp. I don't think we ever loved each other, but she certainly loves my money." He sipped his drink and frowned a bit. "She had nothing in the way of a dowry because of mismanagement by her father. But that is the life of nobility. We marry for duty, not love. How I envy you."

Alvin suddenly realized that being a noble came with its own set of problems and it was true that money can't buy happiness.

Ellinwood slapped the arm of the chair and startled Alvin. "I have it. We'll take everyone outside into the garden for a walk. It is a full moon, or nearly full enough, and I will take the harpies off to the side and you can ask her."

Alvin was stunned. "I..I.."

"Good God, man. She'll never say yes if you ask her like that. Be a man of action. Be that man who rescued a fat lord in the street two days ago."

Alvin looked at Richard in his chair with an enormous stomach that seemed to roll onto his lap.

Ellingwood laughed. "I know I'm fat Alvin. Gluttony is my sin. Now finish your drink and help me out of this chair to set our plan in motion."

Alvin finished the drink and held a hand out to Ellingwood.

Richard snatched it with one hand and braced himself with the other. "On three." Ellingwood rocked forward with each count. "One, two, thrreeee." Alvin pulled him up hard and thought he might fall himself in the process, but Richard was on his feet. "I weight nearly twenty-eight stone."

Alvin's eyes were huge. Twenty-eight stone was nearly four-hundred pounds.

"Perhaps I should walk more and eat less. But the only time I am truly happy is when I am eating and drinking. In fact, I'll take another for the garden." He picked up the bell and rang it again. White was there in an instant. "White. Another cognac for me and have another bottle of champagne brought up. In fact, bring two."

"Yes, my lord. Immediately."

Ellingwood collected the ladies, and the five went outside into the moonlight. The garden was ringed with lilacs in bloom and the evening breeze made the whole area smell dreamlike.

True to his word, Ellingwood took the ladies away, and Alvin led Edna to a stone bench between two lilac trees.

"Are you having a good night?"

Edna crinkled her mouth like she had tasted something bitter. "Mostly. But those two are harpies. They said the most awful things about his lordship. It made me uncomfortable. Then his wife was explaining the finer points of cosmetics as if I would ever be wearing some."

"You don't need cosmetics. You are the most beautiful woman I have ever seen, and I would never want anything to cover your perfect face."

"You're a charmer McGinn. I'll give you that."

"It is a perfect face. In fact, it's the only face I want to wake up to for the rest of my life. And your father has given us his blessing."

"Are you teasing me, Alvin? If you are, I'll be very cross."

He looked into her eyes. "No, I am proposing to you. Such as it is."

He saw tears forming in her eyes and a smile grow across her face. "Yes. Alvin. The answer is yes."

They embraced, and he kissed her for a long moment.

Ellingwood called out from behind them. "White. Bring one of the champagnes please. The other one is for you to take home and share when you tell your families."

Seven

Alvin held Edna's hand as the carriage left the manor house. She held his hand with both of hers and laid her head on his shoulder. "I think I'm going to be a mess tomorrow. That champagne is going to my head."

"Me too. I drank more tonight than I have in the past month. I don't think I could like that lifestyle." They rode in silence for a way, and Edna was already asleep on his shoulder. He leaned his head over and buried his face in her hair. It was so soft that it felt like corn silk on his cheek. He started to drift off himself but was jolted awake by the rough ride over cobblestones as they entered the village.

He sat up and got his bearings. He wanted to talk with her some more, but not with Smith listening in. "Mr. Smith, this will be fine. Just pull in by the church and we'll walk from here."

"Are you sure? There could be miscreants about."

"I'm certain we'll be fine."

"Well, to be honest McGinn. His lordship gave me strict orders to see you both home safely. But I will tell you what I'll do. I'll drop you at the top of the lane and you can see her home. I'll go down to the road a bit and pick you up on the way back. How does that sound?"

"That sounds fair enough." Alvin gently shook Edna awake. "Sweetheart, time to wake up. We're almost home."

Edna sat up and yawned. "I was sleeping so well."

"You'll sleep better in your own bed."

Smith slowed the carriage and stopped at the top of the lane. He hopped down to open the door. "Mind your step, sir."

Alvin climbed down and turned to help Edna. As she stepped down from the chaise, Alvin couldn't help thinking how she looked like a princess tonight and smiled from ear to ear.

Edna frowned. "Why are you smiling like that, Alvin?"

"That's love, Miss." Smith said. "Old men can always tell when young men are in love. And this young man loves you deeply."

"It's true." Alvin said and gave her his elbow. They walked along the lane with her on one arm and the bottle of champagne from Ellingwood in the other.

"I had a wonderful time tonight." Edna whispered.

"Me too. I like his lordship. When we were alone, it was like talking with a friend."

"Huh. He needs a friend with those two lurking about. They kept calling him *his obese-ness*. I'm not sure what that means. But I'm looking it up in my dictionary when I get home."

Alvin thought for a moment. "Let me know too, because I don't think that I have ever heard that term myself."

"They are wicked, and they are harpies. One is obsessed with money and the other consumed with her own beauty. Neither of them really cares about his lordship. I don't think his wife even loves him."

"He told me that they had an arranged marriage. He never wanted her, and she clearly did not want him."

Edna stopped and turned to Alvin. "That may be the worst thing I have ever heard. Why would they do it?"

"Their fathers arranged it. He was doing his family duty."

"That's awful." Edna turned back down the lane, and they continued on.

"What have we here?" they heard a voice call from the shadows. "The Bonney prince and his little princess."

They stopped, and Alvin saw a small man with long greasy hair, emerge from the shadows. He swayed as he walked and held a clay pipe in his mouth. "What do you have there? A drop of wine?" He said and laughed with a raspy laugh from years of smoking.

"Nothing that concerns you. Why don't you go sleep it off?" Alvin said, and they started toward Edna's house.

"Who are you talking to boy? Not me? I don't answer to Bonney princes." The man stepped toward Edna, and Alvin slid between them.

"Go sleep it off." Alvin said and placed his hand on the man's chest to prevent him from coming any closer.

THE ROBIN'S GAZE

The man started to raise his hand and Alvin shoved him hard, sending him sprawling backward hard onto his ass.

"Leave em be. Potts," called another voice from the shadows and a second man stepped forward. He was a little larger and had the tough look of a fisherman. He looked at the couple and waved them on down the lane. "Get going. I'll tend to him."

Alvin and Edna quickened their pace and soon arrived at her door. "Take the champagne. My brother might drink it if I bring it home."

Edna chuckled. "I'll hide it from my brothers as well."

He pulled her close and kissed her. "Goodnight, my future wife. I love you."

She smiled. "Goodnight, future husband. Get that farm going soon. I don't want to live here anymore."

They kissed again, and she went inside.

Alvin was so happy that he nearly floated up the lane. He was smiling as he walked and started to make a list of what he needed to fix the cottage. He was so deep in thought that he didn't hear Potts as he jumped out of the shadows and knocked Alvin to the ground.

Potts was on top of him and struck him in the face. "Empty your pockets Bonney Prince Charlie."

As he raised his hand to strike Alvin again, he suddenly fell on the ground beside him unconscious. Alvin looked up to see Smith standing over him with a short staff that had a ball as big as an apple at its end in one hand and the other extended to help him up. "Did the Miss get home alright?"

Alvin grabbed Smith's outstretched hand and got to his feet. "She did."

"Are you alright lad?"

Alvin rubbed the side of his face. "Yes. He's so drunk he hits like an old woman."

They looked up to see the other man standing in front of them, flanked by a couple others who looked to be fishermen too. "I tried to warn him. Can you be sure to tell Paddy I had nothing to do with it?"

"I guess. But I don't even know your name. He's Potts I take it," Alvin said, pointing to the lump on the ground.

"I'm O'Shea. Dennis. I try to keep him in line, but once he starts with the drink, he can't keep out of trouble."

Alvin nodded. "I'll tell him you had nothing to do with it."

"Thank you." O'Shea took Potts by the wrists and started dragging him into the shadows again.

Smith let his staff slide to a walking stick, and it made a loud pop when it hit the ground. "I'd better get you home before there's any more mischief."

"To be sure, and thank you," Alvin said.

Smith brought him to the McGinn cottage and stopped at the path.

"Don't get down," said Alvin. "I can see to myself."

"I appreciate that," said Smith. "His lordship likes you very much. I hope you'll come to see us again."

"I would like that. But this is my only fancy suit for dinner."

Smith laughed. "Well, come for lunch then."

Dennis sat on a small wooden box beside Potts. The crack on the head knocked Potts out, but he was still alive. He was going to have one hell of a hangover, but Dennis felt he had probably earned it. As he sat smoking his pipe a shadow crept across Potts and he realized that something was blocking the sunlight and not something, but someone. Dennis sat back and raised his palms. "Paddy. I had nothing to do with it."

Padraig stood with his arms crossed, glaring at Potts. "Sean. You and Finn go fetch some river water and get back here." The boys disappeared toward their boat. He looked at O'Shea. "Did he hurt my future son-in-law?"

Dennis seemed confused for a moment then realized that Paddy wasn't joking. "He struck him once. On the side of the face, I think. But he was pretty drunk, and the boy laughed it off."

Paddy nodded, but he wasn't laughing. Sean and Finn returned with a bucket of water each. "Sean, pour yours on his crotch so he looks like he pissed himself."

Sean chuckled and started pouring the water slowly on Potts' crotch. When Potts stirred from thinking that he'd wet his pants, Paddy took the bucket from Sean and threw the rest in Potts' face.

Potts sputtered and tried to clear his face of water. While he was trying to rouse himself to consciousness, Paddy took the bucket from Finn and sat it on the ground beside Potts. He kneeled beside him and grabbed him by the hair and forced Potts' head under the water. Potts struggled, but Paddy Collins was a strong man. After fifteen seconds or so, Paddy ripped Potts' face from the bucket.

Potts made a huge gasp and immediately started coughing. When he saw Paddy, his eyes grew wide, and Collins forced his face back into the bucket. This time Potts was able to upset the bucket and again gasped for air. "Please Paddy." He gasped and coughed. "Please. I'm sorry. I didn't recognize your daughter. I thought they were some rich folks that got lost."

Paddy looked around to see if anyone was watching, then covered Potts' mouth and dragged him behind a row of boxes. He threw Potts to the ground and climbed on top of him, straddling his chest. Potts tried to fight, but he was helpless. Paddy brought his fist down square on Potts' nose. The blood began flowing almost instantly. Collins grabbed him by the face and leaned in. "You leave here today and don't ever come back."

"Where…"

Collins shook him by his head and whispered again. "To-day."

Potts looked at him with the terror that an animal gets just before the slaughter.

"Understand? Today."

THE ROBIN'S GAZE

Potts nodded, and Collins released him. When Paddy stood, Potts grabbed at his nose to try to stop the blood. "I think you broke it."

"Better your nose than your neck. Eh? That was my second choice."

Paddy stood and brushed himself off. When he emerged from behind the boxes, he found O' Shea on his box, chatting with Sean and Finn.

"Fish don't catch themselves, now do they lassies?"

"No, Da," said Sean, and a split-second later Finn answered with "No Da."

The boys jumped to their feet and scurried off to the boat to prepare shove off.

Paddy turned to Dennis. "I don't ever want to see his face around these docks again."

Dennis nodded. "He won't be back."

※ ※ ※ ※

Alvin sat at the kitchen table, rubbing the side of his face and sipping his tea. He didn't notice Ambrose coming into the kitchen. "What happened, son?"

"I'm going to marry Edna."

"Christ, man. And she struck you?"

Alvin laughed. "No Da. It was some drunk from the docks. But the driver from the manor house set him to rights."

"How'd he do that?"

"The driver gave him a knock on the head with an oak staff."

Ambrose nodded and scratched at his stubble. "Well, if he doesn't learn from that, he'll never learn a'tall."

Alvin sipped his tea and smiled. "I suppose not."

Ambrose poured a tea and sat across from Alvin. "So, you say you're getting married, son?"

"I am Da."

"Have you talked to her father?"

"I have and he says as soon as I have the farm going with a place to live, we can marry."

Ambrose pondered on that for a moment and sipped his own tea. "A sensible man. I like him already."

"He's a fisherman from town."

Ambrose smiled. "I know who he is. The village isn't that big. He's a man who loves his family. You could do worse."

"I imagine so."

"Don't cross him, though. He's not a man to be trifled with."

Eight

Alvin stepped up to the door to the three-room cottage. The wood was covered with a thin layer of moss and had a slimy feel when he pushed on it. The door swung open, and he was hit in the face with the smell of decrepit earth and mold. The thatch had rotted through in spots and the dirt floor of the cottage was covered in droppings where birds had made their way in and out over the years.

The windows were all intact, which made him happy, but the years of moisture had swollen the wood to the point that they could no longer be opened. He was adding it to the mental list of fixes needed. A list that was getting longer by the minute.

The one bright spot was that the turf stove in the main room was a little rusty on the cooking surface, but overall, it was in decent working shape. "Well, we'll be able to eat," he said aloud to himself. But then he wondered how he would ever be able to afford to fix everything.

There was a table and two chairs in the corner. When he put some weight on the first chair, it felt as though it might collapse. The second one was already held together with wire, so he didn't even bother to test it. As much as he loved Ireland, one of the things that had always frustrated him was the lack of wood on the island. It forced them to build their houses from stone. They were certainly sturdy in their construction, but working with rock took significantly longer to build or repair anything.

Alvin started piling debris from the roof in the middle of the floor. He thought about trying to sweep the dirt, but somehow that seemed pointless. A flat shovel was what he needed. As he stood contemplating the best way to clear the mess, there was a knock on the door casing.

He heard a voice behind him. "Ewww, it smells."

It was his sister Emily, and she stood with a crinkled face, holding her nose.

Annie scowled and slapped Emily with the back of her hand. "Hush girl. Learn some manners."

She stepped into the cottage along with Jameson and Emily who had let go of her nose and was now rubbing her head where Annie had cracked her.

Annie nodded with approval. "I know it seems like a bit of a disaster, but it's good-sized and has three rooms. You'll appreciate that when your children get older."

Now Alvin crinkled his brow. "I will?"

"You'll appreciate the privacy," Annie said, shaking her head at how dense he could be at times.

Alvin laughed. "I supposed we will. But we won't have to worry about that for some time. This will take forever to rebuild."

"Nonsense. We'll clean it today and you can get the roof mended. When you have that fixed, start running the stove. It will help to dry things out."

He glanced around and shrugged his shoulders. "I was rather hoping to avoid burning up the sod in the summer."

"Then live with the stench. But until you dry this place out, it's not going away."

"I suppose you're right Ma."

"Well, of course I am. Just ask your father and he'll tell you I'm right." She surveyed the cottage and turned to Jameson and Emily. "Jameson, pick up all of this old thatch and make a pile of it outside. Emily, you can help him."

Jameson was eleven and always eager to please. "Yes Ma," he replied and immediately started gathering thatch from the floor.

Emily was ten and scowled a bit as she started to move slowly toward the thatch.

Annie stiffened and took a step toward Emily, "Unless you'd be carin' for a slap on the other side, unscrew your face and move your arse young lady."

Emily picked up an armload of thatch and hurried outside, keeping clear of Annie's reach.

She was the youngest, and there was a nine-year difference between her and Alvin. In the seven-year space between Kellen and Jameson, were three lost siblings. The first had been a miscarriage and wasn't named. The next was Margaret, who died a few days after birth, and then Bridie, who was born two years before Jameson. She was taken by a malignant fever at age five. The loss of three babies in a row made Annie protective of the youngest two, but not so much that they wouldn't be taught proper manners and sound judgement.

After seven pregnancies, Annie had decided that was enough and forbade Ambrose from making her pregnant again. She longed for a baby to hold, just as long as she could hand it back at the end of the visit. That was the beauty of grandchildren.

By the end of the afternoon, the cottage had been cleared of debris and seemed almost livable, as long as you didn't look up at the roof. As they were preparing to leave for the afternoon, they could hear hoofbeats in the distance.

"I hear horses," said Jameson as he stepped onto the road to see what was coming.

Annie grabbed him by the collar and yanked him onto the grass in front of the cottage. "Haven't you got any sense, boy?! Those horses will never see you and run you down. Get the hell out of the road."

A two-horse carriage came thundering down the road and Alvin raised his head to see Smith at the reins. At the sight of the McGinns in the yard, he leaned back and slowed the carriage. The horses were in a state of lather from the run down the road. "Easy boys! Easy!" He called and brought the carriage to a stop.

Smith smiled and jumped down to open the door.

Richard slid out onto the road with a huge smile on his face. "Mr. McGinn. I was hoping to find you here."

Alvin stepped up and shook his hand. "My Lord."

Richard surveyed Annie and the children. "You must be Alvin's mother."

Annie smiled and put the children in front of her. "My Lord. Thank you so much for what you have done for Alvin. We appreciate you more than you will ever know."

Richard smiles and waved a dismissive hand. "Please, Mrs. McGinn, he saved my life you know. Had I died, the Harpies would have taken my fortune." Richard erupted in a laugh that made his jowls jiggle.

"Harpies, My Lord?" She asked with a puzzled look.

"My wife and her sister, Madam. The Harp sisters. Wealth sometimes attracts the wrong type of women. Or men, for that matter," he stroked his chin and looked into the air as if deep in thought, "If I had only been born good looking instead of rich, perhaps I would have found a true love like my friend Alvin."

Alvin felt a little embarrassed by the comment. "My Lord, I'm sure it's not that bad."

"Huh! You met them. They want me to eat and drink myself to death so that she can have my money." He turned to Annie. "You see, Mrs. McGinn. My wife is obsessed with money and her sister is obsessed with her own looks. It's like living with the female versions of Midas and Narcissus. They both tolerate me as well as they can. But truly, they want my money. Not me."

Annie wasn't sure why he was saying all of this, but she did feel bad for him, although she had never seen such a fat man in her life. Clearly, he never went without food for a day in his life. "I'm sorry to hear that my lord." She replied.

"Hah. Thank you. But I'm used to it and in truth, the loathing is mutual." Ellingwood laughed and looked to the McGinn children. "Who are these young ones here?" He asked.

Annie smiled. "This is my son Jameson and my daughter Emily."

Ellingwood stepped over and messed up Jameson's hair. "Strong looking young man." He grinned at Emily. "And a lovely young lady."

Emily tilted her head and focused her gaze. "How did you get so fat my lord?"

Annie gasped so deeply that she might have sucked all the air from the sky. Alvin could see that she was about to strike Emily when the tension was broken by Ellingwood's powerful laugh. "Ha, ha, ha! I ate too much sweetheart. I always eat too much."

Annie reached out for his hand and held it in hers. "Please accept my apologies my lord. The girl may be lovely, but she's obviously a half-wit."

That made Ellingwood laugh again. "Nonsense Mrs. McGinn. I ask myself that question every time I see my reflection."

Annie looked at him with pitiful eyes.

He leaned down and looked at Emily. "And then I get something to eat. Ha, ha, ha!" He stood again and slapped his belly at his own wit.

"Thank you for your understanding, Lord Ellingwood," she said and bowed her head. "We're heading home Alvin. I'll save you some meat and potatoes from dinner."

"Thank you, Ma."

Annie, Jameson, and Emily said their goodbyes and headed back toward their own cottage.

Ellingwood looked over the cottage and his eyes grew big at the amount of work that would be needed to make the place inhabitable. "It hasn't seen much love over the past decade or so."

Alvin laughed. "That she hasn't to be sure."

"Have you thatched a roof before?" asked Richard.

Alvin shook his head. "I've seen it done, but never tried it myself."

Richard squinted as he considered the roof and nodded. "We had a man thatch some of the outbuildings at the manor house. I'll have him come down."

"Oh. Thank you, my lord, but I was going to do it myself to save money."

Richard smiled at Alvin, then called to the driver. "Smith. What was the name of that thatcher from Dingle?"

"Berry, m'lord. Michael Berry."

"Yes, that's right. Berry. I'll have him over to take a look and give you a price, then you can do what you want. You can't beat a man at his trade. A leaking roof might cost you more than his services in the long run." Richard pulled a large flask from his pocket and took a drink. "Ahh," he said and offered the flask to Alvin.

He took a small sip and felt the burn in his throat. "Whiskey?"

Ellingwood smiled. "Yes. Irish whiskey." He took another swallow and tucked it back into his pocket. "In London, scotch is all the fashion. But for pure smooth drinking, nothing beats Irish whiskey." He looked around some more. "Where is the lovely Miss Collins?"

"With her family. Her mother says that Sundays are for church and family."

Richard's face was growing red from the whiskey. "I was raised with a similar sentiment. But my *family* doesn't make it to church here. They sleep too late! Ha, ha!" He held the lapels of his coat and stood up straight. "Why don't you all come to a picnic next Sunday and have her bring her family as well, if they won't part with her for the day? Bring your family as well."

Alvin was started to squirm in place. He inhaled deeply and sighed. "My lord. I appreciate the offer most sincerely and I would never do anything to offend you. But I can't marry Edna until we have a place to live."

Richard smiled. "Of course you're right, Alvin. Getting this place ready has to be your priority."

"Thank you for understanding." Alvin relaxed. He liked Richard, but he still felt nervous around him and never wanted to offend him. Although he was so affable that he was not sure that he could ever offend him.

Richard put his big beefy hand on Alvin's shoulder. "Let's agree to get everyone together before I return to London next month."

"I will. I'm sure they'd all find it grand to visit the Manor grounds."

Richard pulled the flask once more and offered it to Alvin.

Alvin smiled and raised a hand. "I really should be working and that's like to put me to sleep."

Richard put the flask to his lips and took a large gulp. He popped the cover back on to the flask and smiled. "Ahhh. Perhaps I'll nap then on the way back." He motioned a fat hand toward the carriage door and Smith snapped to attention and moved to open it. "I'll look into Berry," he said and with great effort hoisted himself into the carriage. As he settled himself on the seat, he smiled and waved to Alvin. "Home Smith."

Alvin waved as he rode away, then turned and went back inside. When he stepped into the cottage, he was startled by a loud *caw*!

He looked up to see a hooded crow peering down from a beam above his head. The bird titled its head and studied Alvin like it was trying to understand why this man was in its house.

Alvin shook his head and went back to work on cleaning the stove. As he started to inspect the firebox, he stopped and turned to face the crow. "Please don't shit on my floor," he said. The crow tilted its head the other way and stared at Alvin. "Or me for that matter."

Nine

Alvin woke to the sound of rain whipping the walls of the McGinn cottage. Thunder rumbled in the distance, and he pictured himself knee deep in the muck of the bog. *No sense in trying to cut peat in this mess,* he thought. Great, wet drops slammed against the windows in something akin to pounding to get in. He looked over at Kellen who was snoring so loudly that it almost drowned out the storm.

I'm never getting back to sleep, he thought and slowly rolled out of bed. He pulled on trousers and a shirt then crept into the kitchen, trying to be as quiet as possible. No one was up yet, except for him, so he opened the front door enough to relieve himself.

He stood pissing on the flowerbed that stood adjacent to the door. As he did, he closed his eyes and smiled from the relief that comes with emptying a full bladder. It was relaxing.

"Don't let your mother see you doing that."

Alvin jumped and struggled with trying to finish. "Sorry Da, it's raining so hard I'm wondering about a boat to get us to work... and I didn't want to get wet."

"Well, don't let her see that, anyway. The next warm day might smell like the loo outside, and she'll be having us move it again," Ambrose said with a grin.

Alvin buttoned his trousers and tucked in his shirt. "I'm worried about the cottage. The thing smells bad enough. Now I won't get the damp out for ages."

Ambrose started a fire in the kitchen stove and placed a kettle on for tea. "It's just water, son. Fix the roof and that will be the end of it."

Alvin pictured the crows huddled inside, keeping dry and shitting all over the kitchen floor. *Edna would be mortified*, he thought. Then he thought some more and realized that no matter what, she would make the best of it. He appreciated that about her. No matter the task, she just seemed to persevere. "I suppose you're right Da. Lord Ellingwood is sending a man to give me a price to fix it."

Ambrose warmed his hands over the stove. "Thatching is something that, done well lasts a lifetime. If not, it leaks a lifetime. I'm sure this man is good if he did work for the Ellingwoods."

Alvin nodded. "I hope he's affordable." Alvin could feel the damp heighten the stiffness in his back and stretched as much as he could to find some relief. "Are you working today Da?"

Ambrose shrugged. "I don't see the point. We'll be waist deep in the muck by the end of the day."

"Then I think I'll go to the cottage for a bit and then to the village and see Edna today."

Ambrose smiled. "That sounds like a good use of a rainy day. But I wouldn't take her for a walk unless Paddy lets you use his boat to get around."

Alvin pulled a homemade canvas cape from the hook next to the door and threw it over his shoulders. He made it from an old tarpaulin and wore it to keep the rain off. On a day with light rain, it worked pretty well, but on a day like this he'd be lucky if it lasted half-way to town before the rain soaked through.

He wore a wool flat cap that, like the canvas was time limited before soaking through, but he didn't care. He was going to see Edna this afternoon, and that would be worth any annoyance caused by a little rain. First, he wanted to see the cottage to gauge how it was holding up in the weather.

The roof leaked in a number of spots, and he would be happiest when it was repaired. The place had a stench of wet and mildew. Until he could get it heated, he'd try to work with the windows and door open to make the place tolerable.

His calculations were right. About twenty minutes into his walk, he could feel the water seeping through the canvas at every point that touched his body. He shook the big droplets from his shoulders, but it was no use. He was going to be wet.

Maybe I can burn a little of the scrap wood to take the chill off before I go to town, he thought. He had a slice of cold mutton, and a heel of bread wrapped in a cloth for his lunch, but he wasn't optimistic about getting a fire hot enough to boil water for tea. It had been raining for three days straight with barely a break. He wasn't even certain if the wood would be dry enough to burn with so many holes in the roof.

He pulled the canvas higher on his neck and picked up his pace to limit his time in the rain. When he reached the Duffy farm that abutted his property, he saw the owner Sean Duffy leaning on a fence watching a Jersey cow being courted by a Jersey bull.

"Good mornin', Sean!" he called out and Sean turned and squinted through the rain.

"G'mornin', McGinn. Shame about your roof."

Alvin shrugged. "We're going to fix it soon."

Sean nodded. "Well, let me know if I can help in any way. We're neighbors and now we'll have to look out for each other."

Alvin stopped at the edge of the fence and smiled. "Thanks. I appreciate the offer." He looked at the two animals in the pen. "What'd going on here?"

Sean shook his head in disgust and pointed at the cow. "She's in season," he turned and pointed at the bull, "and this lazy bastard doesn't like to feck in the rain I guess."

"I wonder if sheep are like that was well?" he said aloud.

Sean scratched at the stubble on his cheeks. "I don't know. I suspect if they spend enough time together, the ram gets the job done." He looked back at the animals standing facing in opposite directions and both equally disinterested in each other. "These two are like a lot of married couples I know." He laughed and slapped the top of the fence a few times in pure merriment.

Alvin laughed and headed down the road. He turned the corner and saw the cottage in the distance. The sight of it made him smile, and it made him think of Edna. That made him smile even more. Then something caught his eye about the place. The roof seemed odd to him in some way and as he approached, even more so than its usual oddness. He realized that it was lower on one end than the other. He quickened his pace and moved toward the little house faster and faster until he finally broke out into a run. The closer he got; the issue became clearer. A portion of the roof had partially collapsed.

He felt his heart sink like the roof he was staring at.

※ ※ ※ ※

Michael Berry climbed the wooden ladder he brought with him from Dingle. Alvin watched in amazement at the speed with which he made his way around the roof. Berry probed every timber in multiple points with a large, pointed handspike.

When he found a soft spot, he marked it with a number and moved to the next timber.

When he finished, he dropped the spike and chalk into a leather tool bag and walked over to Alvin.

Alvin studied Berry's face, trying to figure out how bad the news would be. "So, what do you think?"

Berry shrugged and scrunched up his face. "I've seen much better."

Alvin could feel the energy leaving his body.

"But I've also seen much worse," said Berry. "Obviously, the problem is here where the roof fell in and it's pretty bad. But the rest of the roof is mostly solid."

Alvin nodded. "I understand. But can you fix it?"

"I can. But it's more complicated than simply replacing timbers and thatch. A roof is a system, and you can't just pull out the rotten parts without some risk to the rest of the roof."

Alvin looked at the timbers trying to imagine how they were all connected. "How do you fix it, then?"

"I'll place a sister timber beside every rotted one and when the frame is rebuilt, we'll pull the rotten wood out. Then we can thatch the roof again."

Alvin tried to imagine what a sister timber was but still couldn't picture it. "How much will it cost?"

Berry started counting the timbers with marks. He stood with his head tilted, looking at the crow that sat on a beam above them as if the crow somehow was assisting with the calculation. Finally, he turned to Alvin and said, "ten pounds."

THE ROBIN'S GAZE

"Ten pounds?" Alvin stood up straight and shook his head as if he had misunderstood the figure.

"Well, three day's labor at two pounds per day and roughly four pounds in timber and thatch. So yes, ten pounds."

"Caw!" the crow called out loudly above them.

Alvin let out half-a-chuckle. "See even the bird is stunned."

Berry shrugged. "It's a fair price, son. I came here because Lord Ellingwood asked me, but if you can do better in the village, then look there."

Alvin suddenly panicked, realizing that he had insulted Berry. "My apologies, sir. I am certain it's a fair price and his lordship thinks highly of your work. Please forgive me if I gave offense."

"No offense taken." Berry scanned the timbers again. "Do you have a large family McGinn? Lots of burly men?"

Alvin crinkled his eyebrows at the question. "There's just three of us. Why?"

"If you get enough men, let's say eight. We could do this in a day. I'd charge you three pounds for the labor and the materials would be the same, but seven is better than ten."

Nearly a third better, thought Alvin. "I can probably come up with six, but I can ask around for a couple more."

"Excellent. Give me a couple of days to get the materials then and we can start work next week."

Alvin smiled and reached out for Berry's hand, "are you a religious man Mr. Berry?" Berry stopped shaking his and gave him a puzzled stare. "Meaning, would you work on a Sunday?"

Berry laughed aloud. "If it pays, the lord will understand."

"That's my philosophy too. Then can we plan on two Sundays from now?"

Berry paused for a moment. "Sure. But I have to have the money for the materials up front. Just send a message when you have the money and then I'll get the timber here."

"Thank you, Mr. Berry. I appreciate your help."

Berry shook his hand again. "Please, lad. Call me Mike. Just make sure you have the men here. Many hands make light work."

"Thanks Mike. I'll do my best."

Alvin sat across the street from the offices of Wilkes and Booth. Seven pounds was not an enormous sum, but it was seven pounds he didn't have. He had committed all of his savings to livestock and had already paid a wholesaler for sheep, chickens and a milk cow, for when the farm was ready.

He took a deep breath and walked across the thoroughfare. *Time to become a slave*, he thought.

Ten

There were no more lines at Wilkes and Booth. Those that could get loans had them now and were hard at work trying not to default. Alvin felt embarrassed to be walking through the door with his hat in his hand like some common beggar who drank away his wages. When he opened the door, a little bell rang to alert the proprietors that they had a customer.

The room was stuffy and the lingering smell of pipe smoke still hung in the air. The counter was empty, and Alvin wondered if they were even open when he heard a voice from the corner of the room.

"Well, well. What do we have here? Young Master McGinn. Are you lost, son, or have you reconsidered trying your luck in America?" Booth was sitting in a chair in the corner. His feet were up on an opened drawer and his eyes seemed to be just waking.

"Neither. I'm here about a loan."

Booth dropped his feet to the floor with a loud thud. "Are you now? That I can help you with." A slight grin crept across his face. "Looking to buy more land?"

"No sir. Fix the land I got. Well, the cottage really."

"Oh, how much do you need?"

"Seven pounds," Alvin said in a voice a little above a whisper.

Booth's grin grew into a smile. "A fair sum. And what would you be using for collateral?"

Alvin titled his head, "Collateral?"

"I thought you were a reader."

"I am. History mostly, I'm not familiar with that term,"

Booth nodded and looked almost fatherly. "Well son, when we give you a loan, you need to put up collateral so that if you default, we get our money back. Do you see?"

Alvin was beginning to understand how the process actually worked now.

"In your case, land would be your best source of collateral. Then you don't have to give us any money up front and when you pay us back, you keep the land."

"How much land would I have to put up for seven pounds?"

Booth produced a book and turned to a page covered in numbers. "Let's see. At one and one-half pounds per acre."

Alvin frowned. "Wait. You offered me two just a month ago. How did you get to one and a half?"

"Well, the price per acre has gone down now, hasn't it."

"It has? I wouldn't know."

Booth gave Alvin a look of derision. "You see, son. There are still large swaths of land unsold on the estate, so the price has dropped to three pounds per acre. So, half of three is one and one-half pounds."

Alvin felt a little deflated. "I see."

"But the good news is that when the land is all sold, the price will rise so your forty acres could be worth much more in the future."

Somehow, that didn't feel like good news to Alvin. As he did the math in his head, he also realized that if he defaulted, Wilkes and Booth stood to make a substantial profit on the resale of any land they acquired. Then he realized that this went for everyone that borrowed from them.

"Alright. How many acres does that amount to?"

Booth ran his finger down the column of the table until he found seven, then ran across until he found one and one-half. He lifted his head and smiled again. "Four and two-thirds acres. But because I like you, we'll just call it four and one-half. You can't argue with that."

Alvin tried to calculate the value and agreed. "I suppose not. What will the payment be each month."

Booth turned to another page in his book and performed the same exercise between column and row. "Eight shillings a month for two years. I wouldn't be comfortable going beyond two years."

"I hope to pay it off before then."

Booth chuckled. "They all do. But don't think of yourself as slave to the lender, think of yourself more of an indentured servant."

Alvin wanted to both laugh and cry at the comment. They had worked their whole lives for rich men and in his dreams, he thought he could be his own man. But now he was simply trading one master for another.

"That's fine. I'll do it. How do I get the money?"

Booth sighed. "You sign a contract son and then I give you the money."

Alvin thought for a moment, "I don't need it for another week or so."

"Then I'd wait til' closer then. Too many of these amadans, as you Irish say, took the loans and the money never made it past the public house."

"That's fine. My Da says that the drink is the death of too many Irishmen."

Booth laughed. "Too many men for sure. But believe me son. It's not just the Irish. Liverpool is full of men who destroyed their lives with drink. It' sneaks up on you like the devil in church. It's just that the people are so drunk, they don't even see him coming."

"Well, I'll be sure to be lookin' for him."

"Good Lad. Come see me next week."

Alvin shook his hand and started for the door then stopped.

"Mr. Booth, can I sign the papers now and pick the money up later?

Booth studied him for a moment. "You can, but why do you ask?'

"Well, the prices on land could change and then I'd have more at risk."

"They could go up, so you'd have less at risk?"

Alvin thought on that for a moment and stroked his chin. "I'm betting they won't. Let's sign the papers now."

Booth laughed, "Don't you trust me son?"

Alvin knew that he could never trust a man like this. He was like the lion on the Serengeti, waiting for the unsuspecting prey. "I do. But I'd rather not take the chance."

Booth grinned and nodded. "I like you McGinn. If you ever want to give up farming for business, come see us. You might just be the brightest lad in this village."

Alvin chuckled. "I don't know about all that, but there is such a thing as being too clever by half, and I want to be just clever enough."

"Well said McGinn. I'll tell Wilkes, that and pass it off as my own."

As Alvin signed the papers, he felt both a sense of joy and dread. It was odd. He had never owed anyone money before, but he had a singular vision. A vision of he and Edna holding a child in the cottage and he'd never get there without a roof.

❋ ❋ ❋ ❋

Alvin stepped into the light fog that was burning off in the mid-morning sun. Even though the sky was cloudy, he was beginning to feel the light heat of the sun and it felt good. His bliss was broken by a loud whistle and catcalling from down the street.

A drunken man with a scraggly beard was leaning against a post with a bottle in his hand. "Hello sweetheart! Have you got anything besides fish for sale?"

An equally disheveled man with tight cropped hair, stood beside him grabbed his own crotch. "I've got a nice eel I'll give you right here lass."

"More jelly than eel, no doubt," cried the scraggly bearded man.

Alvin saw Edna walking briskly up the cobbles trying to ignore them. "Edna!" he called out and her face beamed as she saw his face. She picked up the pace and met her taking her arm. He looked back at the two drunks and thrusts two fingers in the air. The universal sign of piss off.

Enda somehow realized he wasn't at work and stopped. "What are you doing in here in the village?"

"Business."

She frowned skeptically, and pulled her hand away from his elbow. "What kinda' business."

"I needed a loan to set us up in the cottage. Part of the roof collapsed. Do you think Paddy and your brothers would give us a hand a couple Sundays from now?"

Edna grinned. "If it get's him out of church, he'll be there. My brothers too."

"That would be grand. I'm still a couple men short though. I'll have to see what we can do."

Edna rested the basket on her hip and took his elbow again.

"Oh God, please let me carry that." Alvin took the basket of fish and cocked his left elbow out for her to grab.

Edna slid her small hand into his elbow and as they walked up the road, she stood upright as proudly as a queen.

When they had finished selling the catch, they walked back toward town, making idle chatter like couples do and Alvin thought he might be the luckiest man in Ireland.

"I'm hungry," Edna said aloud.

Alvin made dumb show of checking his pockets. "Well, I don't have any food."

Edna stopped dead in the road. "I want an apple."

"The shops will be closed by the time we get back. I can get you one tomorrow."

Edna shook her head and pointed across the stone wall to an apple tree. The tree was surrounded by sheep, grazing in all directions and just beyond the sheep laid a border collie fast asleep.

"Oh. come on Edna can't you just wait until you get home? I can't be seen snatching apples on the side of the road. I'm a respectable businessman now. A gentleman farmer as it were."

"Well, I'm hungry now."

Alvin knew that she was just toying with him. Seeing how far he would go for her. So, he said "the hell with it" and jumped the fence. As he made his way quickly through the sheep they started to bleat, and the tired old collie lifted its head trying to get its bearings. When Alvin reached the tree, he started snatching apples as fast as he could, until the collie barked and sprang to life. Alvin took off in a dead sprint and weaved his way through the herd with his stolen meal in tow.

The collie was incredibly agile and was used to weaving through the herd. It had a piercing bark, and Alvin could sense the dog getting closer.

"Run Alvin! He's going to get you!" Edna called with a great laugh.

As Alvin approached the rock wall again, he tried to judge the distance and leap at the same time. He flung the apples into the road and scaled the fence as fast as he could. He was near the top of the fence when he felt a hard tug at his pant leg. He fought to scale the fence and strained as he took the weight of the dog on his clothing. Alvin felt himself slipping and redoubled his grip before leaping over the wall. He heard a ripping sound and then the sound of the dog started barking again and Alvin landed in a heap on the ground.

Edna doubled over with laughter. "Did he bite you? Or just scare you half to death?"

Alvin jumped to his feet and brushed himself off. As he examined his legs, he saw that the bite had ripped his trousers nearly to the knee.

"He ripped my best pants! That's all."

"Better than your foot. You'd look funny on the end of peat shovel hopping on one leg."

Alvin picked up two apples from the road and shined one upon his shirt. He handed it to Edna. "I hope yours has a big juicy worm in it."

Edna drooped her bottom lip in an exaggerated sad face. "Oh. So cruel."

"Well. I hope you see that I would risk life and trousers to be sure you're well taken care of."

Edna bit into the apple with a loud crunch and talked while chewing. "This is the best apple I've ever eaten…because it was picked with love." Then started laughing again.

Alvin shook his head and cleaned his own apple. "I'm not sure who's more enchanted by your wit. Me… or yourself."

Eleven

Alvin arrived early that morning and sat outside of the cottage on a small bench he had made from two stumps and a board. He hadn't been able to get anyone else to help on a Sunday, but he had sent for Michael Berry, anyway. He sat nibbling on a crust of soda bread, trying to reconcile in his mind how they would remove and replace timbers with so few people.

He looked at the roof and studied the lines. The old thatch looked haggard in contrast to the prefect blue sky. *At least it's not raining*, he thought to himself.

"Are you looking for heaven, son?" Alvin was started from his thoughts by his father's voice.

Alvin turned to see his father and brother walking up the road.

"No. Just trying to figure how so few will be able to accomplish so much. The timbers are large, and the thatch is thick. It'll make for heavy work."

Ambrose grinned. "You'd be surprised how much work a man can do if he puts his mind to it."

Kellen stood next to Ambrose a bit red faced from the walk. "It's not the work that'll get you today. It's the heat."

It was unseasonably warm, and Alvin could feel sweat running down his back, and he hadn't even started working yet. "It's better than rain, that's for certain."

Kellen pulled a cloth from his pocket and wiped his brow. "Can you image when they built the pyramids in Egypt. How did they stand the heat."

Ambrose shook his head. "Good God son. They were mostly slaves. I don't think the builders had much of a care for their well-being."

The conversation was interrupted by the rumble of a wagon coming toward them from the opposite direction. They turned to see Berry sitting atop a wagon heaped with thatch for the new roof. He rode wearing a wide straw hat to keep the sun off from his face and he held a clay pipe in the corner of his mouth.

Berry pulled the pipe from his mouth and looked around. "Ah, young Mr. McGinn. You appear to be several men short of what we talked about."

Alvin flushed a little. "I have more coming. They had to make the journey from the village, but I expect them soon."

Berry pulled the brake on the wagon and jumped down. "How many?"

"Three," Alvin said sheepishly.

"Ah Jaysus lad. It can be done, but it works better with eight. Two pulling down the old roof. Two cutting timbers. Two setting the new roof and two to lug everything about."

Ambrose stepped forward to shake Berry's hand. "I'm Ambrose and this is Kellen," he said with a jerk of his thumb. "I know we're few in numbers but set us a task and we'll get started."

Berry eyed the leather bag of tools that Ambrose had slung over his shoulder. "Are you a carpenter?"

Ambrose chuckled. "Middling at best."

Berry smiled. "Well middling is better than no carpenter at all I suppose."

"I don't know about that. I've seen a fair number of broken shanties built by middling carpenters."

Berry patted Ambrose on the shoulder. "That's what your son is paying me for." Berry pointed at Alvin and Kellen. "You two unload the wagon and your father and I will start to get some accurate measurements.

Alvin and Kellen started toward the wagon and heard the sound of a donkey cart. Alvin looked down the road and saw Paddy and his sons leading a cart with tools.

"Here comes our help," Alvin said with a wide grin when he saw Edna walking with a large basket.

Berry nodded with satisfaction. "Good. That will help to be sure."

Kellen pointed down the road behind the cart. "To be sure is right. Will ya take a look at that?"

Behind the Collins' was Sean Duffy and a half dozen other men, all carrying ladders and tool bags. The sight hit Alvin squarely in the heart and he thought he might actually cry for a moment before collecting himself. It was a small army of men coming to help. Sean had offered to help, but Alvin had no way to pay him, so he couldn't bring himself to ask for free labor, when he had a farm of his own to tend.

"Twelve men son. That's a number I can work with," Berry said with a grin.

Duffy walked up to Alvin and shook his hand. "I expect you could use a few more men."

Alvin nodded and looked at the ground. "I do. I just don't have a way to pay you all."

"You've learned your first lesson of being a farmer. We take care of each other. Some day one of us will need help and I'd hope you'd show up without expecting to be paid."

Alvin blushed at the thought, "of course I would. I mean help, not expecting pay."

Duffy grew serious. "If these farms fail, the money lenders will take the land back and the farmer will be ruined. We need to take care of our own. Now more than ever."

"Thanks... All of you."

Duffy turned to Berry. "Now set us to work."

THE ROBIN'S GAZE

❦ ❦ ❦ ❦

Berry assigned all the tasks. Two teams were assigned to cut the timber and two were busy pulling down the rotted thatch. Everyone was hard at work when another wagon came rumbling down the road with an older white man, a black man and an enormously fat man all crowded onto the bench.

"What's this outfit about?" asked one of the men cutting wood.

Berry smiled. "It's his lordship. Perhaps he's come to lend a hand."

"Huh." said the woodcutter. "He doesn't have hands made for labor."

Berry gave him a reproachful look. "Every man's hands are made for labor of some type."

Smith pulled back on the reins and the wagon rumbled to a stop.

Richard was dressed in working clothes and his riding boots. He climbed down and landed with a loud thump followed by White and Smith. In that back of the wagon sat two women that Alvin recognized as the cooks from their dinner at the manor house.

Richard stepped forward to Berry. "We've come to help, and we've brought some food for the men. A man can't work on an empty stomach." He patted his wide belly with a smile. "God knows I can't."

"Thank you M'lord. Your men can join the teams pulling down the old roof."

"That's fine." Richard pointed to the roof and Smith and White obeyed without question. "But what about me? What can I do?"

Berry was taken aback by the question. "You sir? ... We couldn't impose."

Richard laughed. "Nonsense. I may be fat. But I can still work."

Berry looked around. He looked at the roof and immediately ruled that out. Neither the ladders nor the roof itself were likely to hold his weight. He looked at the woodcutters. "Can you help move the timbers?"

"Of course I can. Better that than standing on a ladder," he said with a great bellowing laugh.

Alvin had been pulling the old thatch off and as he sat straddling a roof timber he looked around. Everyone was busy and the pile of cut timbers was growing by the minute. He saw Edna dragging piles of old thatch and throwing it in the back of Berry's wagon. She was sweaty and covered in dirt, but she looked as beautiful to him as ever. He felt his heart swell with appreciation for everyone helping him.

"Alvin!" He was startled back to the present by the sound of Paddy barking at him. "Stop daydreaming about my daughter and catch the end of this rope when I throw it to you."

Alvin blushed and held his hands out.

"Now catch this so I don't hit you in your heart shaped eyes!"

This brought a chorus of laughter from the other men and Alvin caught the rope, then tied it to the ridge beam that ran down the center of the cottage. He snuck a glance at Edna, and she was silently laughing at him. He smiled and she smiled back. She blew him a kiss and he grinned.

He stepped off from the beam he was sitting on and moved his foot to a support timber below. He felt it sag a little and tried to move back to the ladder gingerly, when he heard a snap and the beam disappeared from under his feet. As he fell, he snapped out with his right hand and caught the rope. The heavy cord was tearing across his palm when he grabbed it with his left. With both hands screaming in burning pain, he loosened his grip and fell to the dirt floor below with a crash of timber around him.

All the wind was knocked out of him, and he struggled to take a breath. Men rushed in to help and when his lungs finally overcame the shock, he gasped and rolled to his hands and knees. His head was buzzing, and he could see people talking to him, but he couldn't hear them. When he finally was able to breathe again, he said, "I'm alright," and held out a hand. Richard grabbed his hand and helped him to his feet.

"Thanks M'lord."

Richard smiled and patted his shoulder.

Berry surveyed the progress they had made and decided now was as good a time as any to eat.

"M'lord. Did you say that you had brought some food?"

Richard wiped his face with a cloth and pushed it back into his pocket. "I did, and we have ale too."

This stopped the farmers in their tracks and greedy smiles swept across the room. Berry could see the problems with that, but who was he to deny a lord.

"Could we limit the ale to one bottle per man until the job is done? We don't want anyone else falling off from the roof."

Richard laughed. "Of course. You're in charge. Let's eat."

Berry had a heel of bread with a slice of cold meat and cheese cradled in a cloth in his right hand and a bottle of ale in his left. He sat down beside Alvin and Edna.

"This your wife to be McGinn?"

A great smile came over Alvin's face, "She is."

Berry studied the cottage. "This will be a will be a grand place to raise a family."

"I'd have lived in a hovel with him, but thanks to his Lordship, we have this place and perhaps we can finally be married."

Berry smiled. "Look around McGinn. You're a very rich man. It's good to have people who care about you."

Alvin's eyes drifted across the men sitting and laughing. Covered in sweat and dust. None of them were being paid. They just did it because someday they may need a hand. Duffy's words came back to him, and he smiled. "We take care of our own."

Twelve

Richard sat on a bench beside a large gazebo with the Harp sisters seated to his left working on embroidery. Under the canopy sat a table full of foods and drinks. To the Collins and McGinns it was the biggest feast they had ever been a part of outside of a wedding. There were meats, cheeses, breads and cakes. Fruits and jellies and cold drinks of the alcoholic and non-alcoholic varieties.

On the lawn in front of the gazebo were croquet wickets set up and ready for play and horseshoe pits. Alvin had seen horseshoes played but had never tried himself. The manor house grounds were dotted with benches, gardens and a pond, all connected by a series of paved pathways. "If I had a penny for every paver here, I'd never need to fish again," said Paddy with a chuckle. "Imagine the poor bastards that had to lay all that stone."

"I've done it before. I never minded laying pavers, but I once spent a year working in the Glentown quarry in Donegal. It was the kind of work that makes a young man into an old one," remarked Ambrose, "But I was happy to have work a'tall."

Paddy nodded. "True enough, it's like a stretch of poor fishing. You get to where you're happy to catch enough to feed your family."

Richard stood and raised his massive arms. "Friends! Welcome! Thank you for coming."

"Of course they came. There's food and drink isn't there." Eliza-Mae hissed under her breath.

"Quiet, woman. These are my friends."

Laura looked at Eliza-Mae, expecting a response. But she put her embroidery on her lap and glared at Richard, and he glared back. She hated conflict of any kind and searched for something to say. "It's such a lovely day. This might be fun," she blurted out to ease the tension.

Richard turned to Laura. "Thank you, Laura. I appreciate your good humor."

Laura smiled and nodded, but when she caught a look at Eliza-Mae's cold dark eyes, she felt herself melting under her sister's gaze. Laura had never sided with Richard before over her sister, but in truth, it was a lovely day, and she was happy to be outside in the sun instead of inside brooding over being in Ireland.

The McGinns and Collins made their way up the path, and Richard smiled to see Jameson and Emily again. He enjoyed watching children playing and someday he expected to have some of his own, but he wasn't sure how they might conceive, since she hadn't spent the night in the same bed as him for more than a year. So, he contented himself with spoiling his nieces and nephews at any chance he could get.

He saw the two children eyeing the croquet set-up with puzzlement. "Have you played croquet before?" asked Richard.

Jameson shook his head "No M'Lord. How do you play?"

Richard pointed to the balls and mallets, "Well, you strike the ball with the mallet and when you get it between the wicket, you get some points and the one with the most points wins. Or something along those lines."

Laura stood up and laughed. "Richard, there is a little more to it than that. May I show them? I love croquet."

"Be my guest. I was never much of a player myself," he said with a chuckle, and Laura took the children over to teach them the game.

Richard stepped forward and kissed the backs of the ladies' hands, then made the rounds of shaking hands with the men. "Do any of you gentlemen play horseshoes?"

"I have a time or two," said Ambrose, "but most of the horseshoes I've ever been around, were still on the horse."

"Ha-ha. That's a good one," laughed Richard. "Well, it is a simple game, but it can be frustrating at times. What do you all say we have a go and draw for teams?" and the men all nodded in agreement. "But first, we have some ale over here," and he walked to the table taking a wooden bucket full of bottles. "We'll have to serve ourselves. White is packing up the household with Smith for our return to England."

"When will you return to Ireland again?" asked Alvin.

"Around Christmas," replied Richard, and opened a bottle of ale. He took a drink and wiped his mouth. "I enjoy spending the holiday here. It's very peaceful, and it reminds me of my favorite Christmas when I was a child, and it was spent here. It's probably why I inherited it when my father passed. I love it here."

"Then what made you want to sell it? The house is magnificent," said Kellen.

"Thank you. But who said I'm selling the house?"

Kellen felt confused. "They said that you had sold the house to a Vicker from Belfast, and he was going to build a protestant church in the village."

Richard took another swallow and nearly spit it out, laughing. "Christ, that would cause a riot, and they'd probably burn the house down."

"They would at that," remarked Paddy. "I don't know where these things get started."

Alvin opened two bottles of ale and handed one to his father and one to Paddy. "I suspect that people make up their own stories to help understand change. It beats waiting around for the truth."

Richard pointed at Alvin. "This is a wise lad here. But the truth is that most of the estates in Ireland are being broken up and sold. It is easier to sell, than to try to manage from afar. My brothers have estates in England, and I have this one here. They live on theirs year-round, but my business affairs keep me in London most of the time, so this is my refuge from the madness."

"Well, we're happy to hear that you'll still be around my lord," said Ambrose. "Your father was a fair man and you certainly are as well."

"He could be ruthless at times, but he was continuing to build the family fortune. I am the third oldest son and my older brothers can carry that burden. I am content to make my own way in the world."

"Sometimes being content is enough," said Paddy.

Richard finished his ale and grabbed another bottle. "I used to worry about what people thought of me, or what they might say. But then I decided that I can't let other people influence my happiness. So, I decided that I will not care what people think." He took a drink and swallowed. "I am fat. I have eyes and I can see. But I am content, and that is what matters most to me."

Ambrose raised his bottle. "Here, here. To being content." He took a drink and puckered a little from the bitterness of the ale. The rest of the men followed suit and drank a toast to contentment.

They played games and laughed. They ate and drank, and everyone seemed to have a pleasant time except for Eliza-Mae who was polite, but never seemed to enjoy herself. Laura however drank champagne and played with the younger children, then took them for a walk by the pond where a family of ducks glided through the water in a smooth line to escape the McGinn children. Laura brought a crust of bread and tore it into pieces tossing them onto the water. The ducks turned and flew back in a flash to gather up the floating treats. She broke the bread with the children and they tossed the bread closer and closer until they could almost touch the ducks.

When the sun was setting, the families gathered to return to the village, and Richard pulled Alvin aside. "I know I said that I would be back for the holidays, but know that I'll make a special trip back for your wedding if we are invited."

Alvin smiled. "You are always most welcome, Richard. I value your friendship more than nearly anything else. I honestly can't thank you enough for your kindness to my family and I."

"It means a lot to me to hear that. When you have the date, bring it here to the house and the caretaker will get a message to me in London immediately."

"I will. Safe travels."

Richard leaned in and spoke in something a little more than a whisper, "I'd settle for swift travels. I suspect my wife may be cross with me."

Alvin chuckled. "She seems cross with you a lot."

"You know something... You're right. I'm beginning to suspect that I might be part of the problem," he said with a laugh.

Thirteen

Alvin stood holding Edna's hand. He turned and looked at her and thought, If I live to one hundred, I will never see anything as beautiful as this again. He felt his heart race and even fought back a small tear. "Are you ready, Mrs. McGinn?"

Edna turned and smiled, then stood on her tiptoes and kissed him on the cheek. "I am Mr. McGinn."

Alvin nodded to his brother Jameson who was tending the door. The boy gave a mighty shove and the doors to St. James' flew open. When the couple emerged into the September sunlight, the guests erupted in a cheer and the sounds of a bodhran drum, and a tin whistle filled the air.

The entire lane had been cleared and long tables and benches had been erected along each side of the street. Cakes and breads were piled on the tables and at the far end, Richard sat beside a small wagon with barrels of ale stacked in the back. It was his contribution to the party, much to Paddy's chagrin. Although he occasionally drank himself, his friends among the docks frequently liked it too much, and he didn't want a drunken dust up to break out in the middle of his daughter's wedding celebration. He moved to the side of the wagon opposite of Richard and stood like a sentinel scrutinizing guests as they took their pours. Anyone looking like they might be nearly drunk or becoming too boisterous received a glare and a quiet warning.

Alvin admired his new father-in-law. He was tough, and he held sway over the fishermen at the docks. The village had constables, but the docks had Paddy to keep the peace. He wasn't a particularly big man, but he had a presence like a guard dog.

When Alvin first met him, he was in his fishing clothes and looked the part of a fisherman. Today, however, he wore his best suit and derby hat and somehow appeared even more intimidating than usual. Alvin watched him and, as if he could feel Alvin's eyes upon him, his gaze met Alvin's. He held up a hand and motioned Alvin over with his finger.

"I'm proud of you, lad. You accomplished more than I ever would have imagined, and you managed yourself."

Alvin gave Paddy a puzzled look. "Myself?"

"You respected my wishes and didn't get her with child before marriage. You're a good lad."

"Well, to be honest. I do respect you and followed your wishes. I know your wrath would have been great, but my ma's would have been far worse. Folks are afraid of crossing you, but they never met with her wrath."

Paddy chuckled a bit, which was the most Alvin had ever seen him laugh. "Actions have consequences, good and bad. Remember that."

"I will."

"And get to work on a grandchild for Ellen. She needs something to occupy herself other than me."

This time Alvin laughed. "My father said pretty much the same thing to me on our way to the church."

Richard sat among the fisherman and spoke as easily as if among old friends. It made Alvin happy to see him enjoying himself, and it would go a long way toward getting the village to see him as something other than the great lord in his manor house. The village respected the Ellingwoods, but his father rarely came to the village and most of the inhabitants blamed him for every failure. If crops were bad or livestock died, somehow, his lordship was to blame.

But with Richard it was different. Ever since Wilkes and Booth set up shop, he came to town more frequently and even visited the public houses on occasion. That was something that his father had never done. It was somehow beneath him to mingle with the unwashed masses.

As Alvin watched him, he noticed the Harp sisters to his left. They looked bored and only spoke with each other. White stood behind them in his uniform, stone faced, waiting to see to any requests. Eliza-Mae wore an expression as if she was passing judgement on the guests. She sat with a posture that tilted her head back and literally looked down her pointed nose at them and Laura seemed to be searching to see if any of the men might be admiring her. If someone made eye contact, she would give them a polite smile and move on in search of her next admirer.

Alvin was startled a little when Edna touched his hand.

"What are you looking at?" she asked.

"His lordship and his harpies. He looks to be enjoying himself and his wife looks as if she were attending a funeral rather than a celebration. I don't understand it."

Edna laughed. "Husband, men could think on it for a hundred years and not understand women. Particularly those types of women. Her Ladyship judges everyone to ensure that she holds a level of superiority over them. Even her own sister. Laura is constantly seeking admiration for her own self-worth. Can you imagine a London ball with scores of women like the Harps in one room? I don't think I could bear it."

"I suppose it's like that for men as well. That's probably why the nobility has so many titles. Then there is no question of a pecking order."

Enda nodded. "I'm sure you're right. Look at poor Mr. White. Not only does he have to stand there like a statue. He has to listen to their spiteful gossip."

Alvin watched him, standing silently as if he was an object, instead of a person. Alvin actually felt some admiration for him.

His job may not have been a desirable one, but he did it very well. What impressed him the most was his self-discipline to be able to wait patiently for hours on end without even the slightest appearance of discomfort.

Edna picked up a plate with an assortment of cakes and walked to White. "Mr. White, would you be carin' for a cake? They are very tasty?"

Before he could answer, Eliza-Mae waved a finger at Edna and leaned forward. "The servants eat later. In their own area. It's structured that way."

Richard turned and frowned at his wife. His enormous face was flushed from drinking and sweat gleamed on his forehead. "That is nonsense. We'll be here for hours. He can eat whatever he wants. In fact, he can have some ale as well if he wants." He turned to White. "Do you want some ale or something to eat?"

White stood and gently turned his head to Richard and nodded. "No. Thank you, my lord. I ate before we left."

"Well, if you change your mind, you may help yourself. After all, this is a celebration."

Edna smiled at White and walked away with her cakes.

Eliza-Mae leaned toward Richard and spoke in something akin to a harsh hiss. "Honestly Richard. You forget yourself. You forget your position. You are nobility, for God's sake. Try to remember that."

Richard stared into her eyes and filled a mug with ale. He drank it down in one continuous gulp while keeping his glare set into her dark eyes. When he finished, he banged the mug down on the table and startled her. His eyes stayed fixed on hers without blinking. "Smith!"

Smith hurried toward Richard and presented himself. "Yes, my lord."

"Please take her ladyship back to the manor house. Her sister too if she wishes. I believe I will be here for some hours yet, but please return once they are settled."

"Right away my lord."

Eliza-Mae rose and pursed her lips as if she was about to explode in a verbal tirade, but then stiffened and composed herself. She exhaled, nodded to Richard and turned toward the carriage without a word. She stopped and scowled at Laura. "Are you coming?"

Laura hesitated for a moment but felt the full weight of her sister's stare bearing down on her and slowly rose.

"Feel free to stay," Richard said in attempt to needle Eliza-Mae a little more. "These are good people; you might actually enjoy yourself if you can crawl out from under her shadow."

Laura demurred for a moment then spoke in a soft voice. "She is my sister."

Richard raised his eyebrows in a look of surprise at the nonsense of the statement. "Oh, I am well aware. But perhaps someday you will be a person yourself and not just the younger sister of Eliza-Mae Harp."

He could see on her face that she yearned to be her own woman, but he knew that since her mother's death, Eliza-Mae had taken it upon herself to teach her how to be a lady. Eliza-Mae studied and commented on her every move and now she felt so self-conscious about every decision, that she had difficulty making any. Laura dropped her gaze and followed her sister to the carriage.

When the carriage pulled away, Richard turned to the fishermen and smiled. "Well at least she won't be harping on about my drinking. White!"

White jumped to attention and presented himself. "Yes, m' lord."

Richard filled a mug with ale and handed it to White. "Drink it. And get something to eat. We'll be here for some time yet."

"Yes, m' lord." White brought the mug to his lips and swallowed a mouthful of ale. He hadn't realized how thirsty he actually was, and the cool brew felt good on his parched tongue.

Richard smiled. "Please take a seat and drink like men, we're amongst friends, so let's dispense with all of the undue etiquette."

White sat and relaxed. He even managed a smile from time to time as the men laughed and told jokes.

The carriage stopped at the top of the lane, and everyone heard Eliza-Mae's voice. "Get out then!" Laura emerged before Smith could dismount and Eliza-Mae yelled out again, "Drive!" Smith started the team up the street as fast as he dared for fear of running someone down.

Laura made her way back to the table and sat beside White smiling without a word. She looked proud. Like she was her own woman.

Richard handed her a mug of ale and nodded without speaking. He was actually proud of her for standing up for herself. He looked into his own nearly empty mug when he felt as though he was being watched. He lifted his head and saw Edna back at the table with Alvin and she looked at White and then back at him and smiled. He chuckled silently to himself and thought, *what a remarkable young woman. She can bring a lord to his knees with just a smile. I may be a lord, but McGinn is the richest man in this village.*

Fourteen

Ever since the wedding, Alvin had been floating on a cloud. She was his wife, and he was her husband. It would be that way for the rest of their lives. They had planned a trip away from the village and away from the cottage. Alvin's brothers had agreed to tend his small flock of sheep and the keep the foxes away from his henhouse while they were gone.

Richard had secured a small cottage in Castlemaine for a few days as a wedding gift. Although the entire train ride took little more than an hour, the trip was like something of a fairytale for them. Neither of them had even ridden on the train. They had seen it pass thousands of times, but their lives had been centered within the immediate village.

When they arrived at Castlemaine station, a black post-chaise being pulled by a white horse was waiting at the entrance as Richard had instructed and they were to look for a driver named Fitzgerald.

Alvin carried a travel case they had borrowed from a neighbor in one hand and cocked his elbow with Edna's hand on the other arm. As they approached, the driver smiled and jumped to attention. "Would you be the McGinns?"

Alvin smiled, "We are. Would you be Fitzgerald?"

"Aye, Fitzgerald himself."

Edna chuckled, "Fitzgerald himself. Are you famous?"

Fitzgerald laughed and bowed. "I am, miss. I descended from the Fitzgeralds that once owned the castle that Castlemaine is named for. But the castle was torn down long ago. Perhaps they should just call it Maine now. Haha, like in America."

"I know a family who moved to Maine. They sent a letter saying that in the winters the snows are so heavy, it piles up taller than a man," said Alvin.

Fitzgerald looked at Alvin in disbelief. "Taller than a man? How do they get anywhere? The horses must be up to their necks in snow."

"I don't know. Perhaps they stay in one place until spring."

Edna looked at the two of them. "I doubt they get all of that snow at once. It probably comes a little at a time and maybe they pack it down for sleighs like in Russia."

Fitzgerald pointed at Edna. "This is a smart lass, right here. You be sure to keep her close. She's both beautiful and brilliant."

"I plan to," replied Alvin with a grin.

Fitzgerald stepped to the door and opened it with a sweep of his hand. "Leave the bag and step up. You first miss." He extended his hand and took Edna's, guiding her up, "and you sir, mind your step."

Alvin stepped in and plopped down beside Edna. Fitzgerald shut the door and secured the travel bag to the back of the wagon. He jumped on to the driver's seat and started the big white horse with a click of his tongue. While they rode through town, Fitzgerald pointed out sites of local interest. "The Castle House Inn is the place to get a bite to eat. They might cost a bit more, but the cook is a particular friend of mine, and you tell her you know Fitzgerald, she'll be sure you don't leave hungry."

"Thank you. We'll do that... wait, what's your first name?" asked Edna.

"It's Lewin, miss."

Edna smiled. "Oh, I have never heard that before. I like that name."

"Well, my father's father was Lewis Fitzgerald, so were his older brother's son. So, since Lewis had been taken, my father arrived at Lewin."

"It's a grand name to be sure," she said with a smile.

"Why thank you, miss."

Upon arriving at the cottage, they found a basket by the door, concealed by a cloth decorated with embroidered thistles and shamrocks. Fitzgerald opened the door and Edna stepped down and lifted the cloth. A variety of breads, cheeses, butter, and jams were inside, along with some smoked salmon and a round ham roast. Richard had given it as part of the gift, along with a bottle of the champagne they had enjoyed at the Manor house tucked inside.

"Well, you must have some excellent friends McGinn, to be treated so well," remarked Fitzgerald.

"The very best friends," replied Alvin.

The cottage was charming and much brighter than their own. It made Alvin wonder about getting more windows somehow. The minimal number of windows made their home easier to heat, but what he saved on peat, he spent on lamp oil and candles. This cottage also had two doors, which was something he had rarely seen. The doors here opened to the front and to the back through a small anteroom for wet boots and clothing.

"Alvin. I want a room like this at our home someday. Then the barn clothes can stay outside and not smell up the house."

"Well, we're farmers. Our house smells like a farm."

Edna scowled and put her hands on her hips. "I grew up in a house of fishermen and had to tolerate that dreadful smell every day of my life until today. I don't want to trade one form of stink for another."

Alvin grinned. "I'll see what I can do. I live to serve you."

"Well, see that you do. Let's take some bread and cheese for a picnic by the river."

THE ROBIN'S GAZE

"We can on one condition," he said. "I saw a rod by the door. Show me how to fish."

Edna laughed. "Well, that's probably illegal. You need to be licensed to fish the rivers."

Alvin wrinkled his brow like she was pulling his leg. "Lots of people catch fish on the river and no one is ever arrested for poaching. Hell, I have before."

"That's because the old Lord Ellingwood never cared and Richard has never enforced his rights, either."

Alvin laughed aloud. "You know the first time I met Richard; he accused me of poaching his fish and his father sent him away. Now, all these years later, I find out he was right. It's strange how life works."

"It is. I can't show you how to fish, but if there's a hidden away place down there, I'll show you some other things." Edna winked and ran out the door. Alvin chased after her and she called out. "What about the picnic?"

"We'll eat later," she replied.

He caught up to her at the riverbank, pulled her to him and kissed her. She tried to pull away in play, but then her body relaxed, and she kissed him back.

He looked into her blue eyes, and they seemed to almost sparkle. "That was lovely Mrs. McGinn."

"Yes, it was Mr. McGinn." Edna looked across the river in both directions and saw no one around. "Take off your clothes."

Alvin felt panicked and glanced around to see who was watching. "Here? I thought I saw a robin. What if it's your Gram watching?"

"Yes. Here on the grass. Gram is back at the village. She wouldn't fly here, and we waited long enough." Edna unbuttoned the top of her shirt, and when he saw her bare cleavage, he tried to shut her shirt. "What if somebody sees us? There's probably a convent in the village."

Edna laughed. "You need to get out of your wet clothes."

"Wha..."

The moment he opened his mouth, she shoved him backward into the water. He went under and burst to the surface with a gasp! He saw Edna standing on the bank laughing. "I can't swim!" He splashed around and started floating away with the current. Edna stopped laughing and ran into the river, then dove in and swam to catch him. She grabbed his collar and pulled him to the surface, where he gasped again.

He flailed at the water and clung to her, nearly out of breath. "I can't swim."

She shook him by the shoulders, "Okay then. When I say go, stand up. Go!" She jumped up taking him with her and stood chest deep in the water. Alvin looked to see that the water only came a little above his waist.

"Are you okay, love?" she asked.

Alvin frowned. "I might have drowned you know. You didn't know how deep the water was."

Edna looked at him with disbelief. "I spent my whole life on the rivers and the ocean. I have ways of knowing."

"But not on this one. How could you know here?"

Edna pointed down. "Because I could see the bottom was only a couple of feet down. I didn't expect you to float away in knee deep water."

Alvin laughed. "It seemed much deeper at the time. Also, this water is moving faster than it looks."

Edna looked at the river and saw a large rock a little way away. "Come with me." She grabbed his hand and waded out toward the rock. She checked each step as the water rose until it reached her neck.

"Edna, we should go back." Then she started to rise from the water as she stood on a rock and slid herself behind the rock on opposite of the flow of water and Alvin joined her.

"What are we doing?" he asked.

"I'm showing you a secret of fishing. Duck under and open your eyes and tell me what you see?"

Alvin looked with apprehension.

"I won't let you go. I promise."

Alvin took a deep breath and ducked under the surface. Edna held his shirt tight so that he wouldn't slip away. After a half a minute, he popped up and gasped. "Fish!"

"I thought so," she said. "Fish rest behind big rocks so that they don't have to fight to swim upstream all day long. They rest there at night. If you can reach the big rocks, that's your best chance to catch them sleeping in the morning or evening."

"That's amazing. Did Paddy teach you that?"

"Of course. I have only heard it a few...hundred times. So, if you find yourself in swift waters, find a big rock to rest behind. You may be able to swim out and save yourself."

She looked at the shore. "Now let's swim back to the shore and we can get out of our wet clothes. You can warm me up."

Fifteen

Edna loved the Christmas season. People were in good cheer, and it was the time of year that they ate the least amount of fish. At Easter they had ham and after the forty days of lent, that was a welcome treat. Some years they had spiced roast beef, but her mother boiled it and Edna often found the meat both tough and dry. This year Paddy had said they'd be having a goose and had already paid for half of it to ensure that one would be available.

She had been crafting decorations for the cottage. A cedar tree stood across from the cottage and that was the base for all of her decorating, since it was the only evergreen close by. She gathered bows and tied them with a dark twine into a wreath. When she and her brothers were younger, Paddy brought them to the country, and they gathered evergreen branches wherever they could find them and made wreaths to sell around the village.

Paddy liked the ones made from holly, but the kids found them to be hard on their hands with all the points and stiff edges. His hands were leathery and calloused from years of hauling fishing lines and nets, so he seemed to be immune from the pokes of the holly leaves. Enda liked the look of the holly better since it held its color and shine for weeks, but it wasn't easy to find around the village.

The wreath was decorated with clusters of holly berries and any other red berry she could find around the cottage. Her mother had given her a skein of red yarn, and Edna spent her evenings knitting a small red band that she would use of a bow. Knitting long strips of yarn was the first thing she learned to knit as a girl. That's where she mastered the knots that made up the Collins family pattern for blankets and sweaters.

She gathered several sparse looking cedar bows that were still pliable enough to bend and wove them into a cradle like the one that had for their nativity when she was a child. They had figures of Mary, Joseph, the three wise men, and of course Jesus, carved from wood. The nativity was set up under the tree each year and Jesus was added on Christmas morning. She would start a nativity for their home with Jesus in a crib and add on from there.

She liked all the Christmas traditions in her family. The one she has never tried however was the Christmas day swim. It had been a tradition in Ireland for more than one-hundred and fifty years. Paddy had done it and so had her brothers, but Edna wasn't fond of being cold and the tradition in the village was

THE ROBIN'S GAZE

for the men to race to the reef marker and back. She was certain that would lead to being in the water far longer than would be comfortable and no woman had ever done it, but she felt like someday she would be the first.

She was one of the few girls who regularly went out on the boat to fish, and she had beaten both of her brothers in races more than once. It was a point that Paddy liked to bring up whenever one of his sons wasn't working fast enough. He would light his pipe, take a drag and exhale. Then use the pipe as a pointer while he berated them. "Let me see what your sister is up to this afternoon. Maybe you two should sell the fish and we can let her catch them. She's a better fisherman and swimmer than the likes of two of you, Amadans."

Thankfully, her brothers never held it against her. Paddy was how he was. His idea of praise was not to criticize, and he was fond of pointing out that you'd never be praised for "things you're supposed to be doing in the first place."

The next day was December 8th, the day that most everyone in Ireland decorated for the holiday. Trees and other adornments went up, and every house on their lane had a tree visible in the front window. Edna placed her decorations on the wall and the little woven crib under the wreath. We can start our own nativity with that, she thought.

When Alvin came in from the working in the barn, he had six eggs cradled in the front of his shirt. "These will make for a nice pudding for tomorrow."

"Huh. Well, if we're making a pudding, we'll make it with what we have. We're missing a fair number of ingredients."

Alvin grinned. "Don't you worry, love. I've seen me Ma make a hundred puddings. As long as we have bread, sugar and eggs, we can throw anything in we want."

"I like to follow the recipe. Then I know it will be edible," replied Edna.

Alvin placed the eggs in a bowl and pulled her tight, kissing her forehead. "If it's awful, we'll leave it here and I'll eat it. We can tell them we dropped it."

Edna frowned. "Lying is a sin you know."

"It doesn't say that in the bible."

"What about bearing false witness?"

Alvin laughed. "That's against your neighbor, not foul pudding."

"It's the same thing Mr. McGinn, and I won't be a party to your deception," she said with a smile.

"That's fine. I'll tell everyone you made it yourself then," he replied with a mischievous grin.

Edna shook her head. "I'll make sure it's good and if it's not, we'll do better on Christmas day when we have all the ingredients."

He looked at the decorations on the wall and smiled. "Those look lovely, darling. Do you have a baby for the crib?"

"No, not yet. I'm working on it," she said, pointing at a pile of yarn and a half-formed doll.

"I can start making some of the other figures out of wood and we can have a proper nativity of our own."

"That would be grand. But don't worry about it for this year. We can just start with the baby. Maybe Mary and Joseph too, if you can. After all, Jesus can't be an orphan."

"I'll get to work on it," he replied and kissed her again.

***

After midnight mass, Edna spent Christmas Eve with her parents. She had agreed to help her mother with the cooking, so it made sense to spend the night there rather than travel back to the cottage in the dark only to return in the morning.

Alvin had returned home without attending church to tend to the animals. The cow had to be milked twice a day, and they all needed to be fed. When he returned in the morning, he brought a gallon of milk and a dozen eggs. As he walked down the lane towards the Collins' house, he could hear a ruckus inside. He opened the door to everyone frantically searching for something.

"What's amiss?" He asked Edna.

"Baby Jesus is lost." Edna pointed to the mantle. "He was here last night and now no one can find it."

Ellen stood with her hands on her hips. "I don't know what we'll do. What kind of nativity has no Jesus?" she said and made the sign of the cross. "Edna. Do you have any ideas of what we can do. We need a new baby for the crib."

"I think I do Ma." Edna produced a package wrapped in a cloth. When she unwrapped the cloth, she pulled the cedar crib she had made along with the knitted doll, complete with a tiny blanket in the Collins family pattern.

She kneeled and placed it in the nativity next to the original crib. "I haven't learned the McGinn pattern yet."

Alvin smiled. "That's okay. I don't know that I have ever seen it, anyway. Besides, the Collins blanket is a good one for the baby Jesus."

Edna stood and looked at the doll in its crib. "I know it is, but Jesus is here." She reached into her skirt pocket and held the wooden Jesus they had used for years, then pointed to the one she had made. "That's baby McGinn."

Alvin stood in confusion, trying to understand what she was saying. "Why are there two?"

Paddy sighed. "You're a bright lad McGinn, figure it out."

Then it finally clicked in his mind, and he turned and looked at Edna. She was beaming and looked as if she might burst with excitement.

"You're carrying my son?" he said with a grin.

"No. I'm carrying our daughter."

He rushed to her and picked her up in his arms, and kissed her. "How do you know it's a girl?"

"I just know somehow. I'm usually right."

Alvin kissed her again and put her down. "You're always right."

Sixteen

Edna sat at the table with a gallon crock and a wooden ladle skimming cream from the top of the morning's milking. Alvin had added a barrel churn to his list of farm items the next time he sold wool, but for now she was stuck with a crock and a dasher. A wooden stick with a cross mounted to the bottom that pounded the cream into butter. The process always started off easy, but the constant up and down motion made her arms tired.

She tried not to peek at the butter until she felt the right amount of resistance to each plunge. There was something discouraging about looking into the crock and realizing that there was still a lot of work to do. When she arrived at the perfect consistency, she squeezed the ball out with a cheesecloth and pressed it into a mold that Alvin had made. The mold was a simple wooden box with a shamrock and a thistle carved into the top plate, so that when the butter was removed from the mold, a raised version of the carving would be present on the surface.

THE ROBIN'S GAZE

They had seen something similar in Castlemaine, and Alvin felt like it was a simple thing to give their butter a personal touch.

When she finished making butter, she went outside to tend to her daffodil beds. They were one of her favorite flowers because of their early bloom in February and March. She had dozens of flowers read to bloom and pulled the weeds that threatened to engulf them. There really wasn't much chance of weeds actually bothering the Daffodils, but she hated the look of a messy flower bed. When she grew up in the fishing lane, no one tended to any type of gardening, and she was in awe when she walked through the countryside selling fish and saw all the amazing gardens.

One benefit of the rain was the ability to grow most any plant. Once a man from the village brought two small palm trees back from a trip to from Africa and planted them in front of his house and they grew. Edna had heard of palm trees growing in Ireland, but she had never seen one. The man who grew it said that someday, it might produce a coconut or two. But it never did.

As she picked weeds, she saw a robin come hopping toward her. It stopped several feet away and pecked at the ground a little in search of bugs or worms. "Good morning Gram." She said aloud. "Did you hear about my daughter? I suppose Ma told you all about her."

The robin hopped along intent on finding something good to eat and didn't pay attention to Edna. She pulled a clump of weeds and shook the soil out and back into the garden. A short, fat earthworm fell out with the soil and Edna plucked it up and flipped it to the bird. The Robin hopped back and was about to take flight when it realized what was on the ground. It ran to the worm and snapped it up in its beak. In a matter of a few seconds, the worm was gone.

The bird moved closer as if it were looking for another handout. "I'm sorry Gram. If I see another one, I'll send him your way." The bird flew to the windowsill and watched Edna work. She stopped and flexed her swollen fingers and wiggled her swollen toes. She felt like she was drinking too much water and it was making her hands and feet swell, but she constantly felt thirsty. The more she thought about it, the thirstier she got. Edna kneeled on all fours and forced herself to stand. The sudden movement made her feel a little lightheaded, and her arm shot out to brace herself against the doorframe. The robin darted from the window to the safety of a tree branch at Edna's sudden movement. "Sorry Gram. Didn't mean to give you a start. This baby makes me weak in the knees already. Can you imagine when I actually get to hold her?" She laughed as she regained her balance and picked up a bucket to bring water from the well. On her way back to the house she felt a stab of pain in her abdomen and doubled over nearly dropped her bucket. The pain passed as quick as it began and she rubbed her now showing belly. "We'll have your Da fetch the water from now on little one. It's becoming apparent that I'm not as strong as I used to be."

❦ ❦ ❦ ❦

Edna was sitting in her chair knitting when Alvin returned from the village. He stepped into the little cottage with a hand behind his back and a wide grin across his face. "Close Your Eyes. I have a surprise for you."

Edna put down her knitting and closed her eyes. "Oh God, please let it be a barrel churn."

Alvin laughed. "It's better than that," and he placed a bundle on the table.

"Better? Now I actually am excited."

"Open your eyes."

Edna opened her eyes to see a sizeable object wrapped in cloth and bound by a belt. "What is it?"

"Open it," he said almost giddy with anticipation.

Edna opened the bundle to see a stack of books. "Books? How is that better than a butter churn?"

Alvin shook his head. "They are stories for the baby. Richard gave them to us. There are some for us too, after all Dracula is in there and that might scare a child to death."

"It might scare me to death," she said with a chuckle. "But that was very nice of him."

Alvin leaned forward and kissed her cheek. "How was your day, love?"

Edna shrugged. "It was alright, but I'll need you to carry water for me before you go. I'm having a hard time hauling the water. Today I felt a pang in my side so strong I nearly dropped the bucket. It went away in a few seconds, but it was painful all the same."

"Of course. I'll be around here tomorrow to help more." He reached out and took her hands. He could feel the swelling and looked down in shock. "My God Edna. Do they hurt? Your hands are so swollen."

"Not really. My fingers are just stiff, and my skin feels stretched. My feet too. But they get better when I put them up."

"Well, I'll fix us up supper and you can put your feet up while I read you one of these books after we eat."

Edna smiled. "You're a good man Mr. McGinn."

"Thank you, love."

She moved her knitting to the basket, making way for supper. "Not Dracula though. I know it was written by an Irishman, but I want something more fun and less terrifying."

"I have the perfect book. It's called the Adventures of Huckleberry Finn and Richard said it's about a boy on a river in America."

She leaned back and smiled. "That sounds grand."

Crack! They were startled by a loud bang against the window.

"Christ! What was that?" Alvin sprang to his feet and rushed outside. A bird was laying on the ground twitching. It had flown into the window and broken its neck.

"What is it?" Edna asked from the door.

"A bird."

She gasped a little. "Not Gram I hope."

Alvin shook his head. "No. It's a Druid."

"A Druid?"

"Some call it a Starling." He picked up the still shaking bird and brought it to the hedgerow across the road from the cottage and laid it in the thick tangle of branches.

"That's a bad omen, Alvin."

He turned and kissed her cheek. "That's an old wives' tale, and you're a young wife. Don't believe those silly superstitions."

Edna frowned at his dismissive attitude. "They get passed down for generations, so there must be some truth to them somewhere."

That evening, Alvin read the Mark Twain book for a couple of hours while Edna knitted and rested her feet on the little stool with the pillow. When she finished the skein of yarn, she yawned. "That's all for me, I think. Can you help me stand? My knees are stiff from sitting so long."

Alvin stepped over and held her hands. "On three. One...two...three." She leaned forward, and he pulled her to her feet, and she clutched at him to keep her balance.

"Whew. You're so strong, you're making me swoon McGinn," she said with a laugh.

Alvin smiled, but he wasn't sure that everything was alright. "I'll ask Mrs. Duffy to stop by. She's a Handywoman, you know?"

"She delivers babies?"

"Yes, Duffy told me she has delivered most of the children on the farms along this road between here and the village."

"Well, she sounds like a *handy* woman to have around, to be sure."

Seventeen

Edna slid a turve of peat into the stove and blew gently on the coals. The peat smoked, and each breath made the embers glow, but the peat wouldn't ignite. The kitchen was starting to become smoky and she turned her head after each attempt to keep the acrid smoke from stinging her eyes. As she fanned the smoke away, she felt the baby kick hard inside of her.

"I know wee one. I don't like it either," she said aloud. "Your Da should have loaded the stove before he left this morning." She turned her head and took a deep breath of clean air then faced the coals and blew a long, steady breath through pursed lips into the coals. The peat billowed smoke and then ignited. Instantly the smoke vanished up the stovepipe and was replaced by light flames and wonderful heat. Edna closed the door to the firebox and stood, rubbing her belly. "Only two months left my lovely. You'll be born in June so you can enjoy the wee but of sunshine we get here."

She ladled water from a bucket into a small teakettle and placed it on the stove. Her mother had always taught her that the key to good tea was hot water, boiling hot. She spooned out some tea leaves into a warming pot and waited for the kettle to boil. As she waited, she tried to occupy her mind. Edna found that watching the pot seemed to make time stand still, so she cut a wedge of soda bread and smeared it in butter. It was one of her favorite things. She loved the creamy salty taste of butter made at home. They had a Jersey cow, and she gave a small amount of milk each day, usually just shy of a gallon, but it was rich with cream, and it always made the best butter. Many women talked of cravings for different foods. Some craved sweets and some craved sour foods like pickles, but Edna craved butter. Butter on scones, butter on bread, butter on potatoes and even butter on eggs. There was something about the taste and the texture that made her feel good inside. They had butter growing up, but it was something that was used sparingly. By having it here on their farm in a more or less limitless supply, she found herself gorging on it.

She was putting on weight with the pregnancy and she felt that maybe it was more than she should, but Alvin loved how she felt and said that she was growing into her woman's body, and he loved her just the way she was. The part that bothered her the most was the swelling in her feet. Sometimes her feet felt so heavy, it was like walking in mud. Angela Duffy had been to see her and advised her to rest more and lay down when she can.

But Edna grew bored lying in bed and felt like she needed tasks to keep her mind occupied.

The kettle began to whistle softly, and she removed it from the heat. Edna enjoyed the smell of tea as she poured the boiling water over it. There was something comforting about it to her, something that made her feel safe like in her childhood. She poured her tea into a porcelain cup arrayed with a chain of shamrock and thistles that they had received as a wedding gift. It was part of a tea set with service for four and Edna liked to bring it out when her mother or mother-in-law came to visit. Edna made Alvin drink his tea from an old, cracked set that was handed down by his grandmother. Most of the pieces had been broken over the years and he had glued his cup together enough to hold a cup of tea. She wasn't about to take any chances with her new tea set. She wanted to hand it down to her daughter someday.

She was convinced that the baby was a girl and Alvin, of course knew it was a boy. She sat in the chair and put her swollen feet up on a small stool Alvin had fashioned from some straight branches and an old board. It wasn't much to look at, but she liked having her feet off from the ground. She picked up her knitting where she had left off on the baby's blanket. She was knitting in the pattern of the Collins clan with a wide row of lattice knots, flanked by a row of wide diamonds. It was the pattern that she had known best. As a child, she and her mother knit sweaters for her father and brothers to wear while fishing and she could roll through the patterns without looking while her mind drifted to the baby and what names they might choose. They had arrived on Patrick for a boy. It was similar to her father's name, but people would be less likely to call him Paddy. If it was a girl, she loved the name Nora. Alvin liked Brigid, after his sister that had died, but he would do whatever made her happy. It was what she loved about him the most.

As she knit, dreaming about the baby, she tried to flex her fingers. They looked like fat little sausages. *I need to stop with all this butter*, she thought, *or this baby is going to be three parts cream*. She was making salted mutton and barley stew for dinner. It wasn't much to look at and the smell of mutton often made her stomach turn, but Alvin loved it, particularly on cold wet days. And as they had an abundance of sheep on the farm, it tended to grace the menu with great frequency.

She laid her knitting on the table and went to the little cabinet that served as a pantry. On the floor of the cupboard was a series of crocks, each filled with salted meat. She lifted the heavy cover of the salted mutton, and the smell hit her so fast that it seemed to make a direct course to her stomach, and she belched a little as she fought back, vomiting. Edna looked away as she reached into the cloudy murk and pulled a cut from the bottom. "God that's foul," she said aloud. "This crock has no end to it. We'll be eating the same salted meat on your first birthday wee one." Directing her words to her belly, the baby turned and kicked as if in agreement with her.

"Ooof. I see you don't like it either," she said with a soft laugh. The laugh sent her into a fit of coughing and she felt a

THE ROBIN'S GAZE

wet rattle in her chest. She grimaced as the coughing led to a burning in her throat. She sat back down and caught her breath. "I guess I need some rest, Nora. Your Da might have to wait for his supper tonight. That meat is going to need a long boil before it's fit to chew."

Edna sipped her tea, and her hand began to tremble. She slid the cup and saucer back to the table and pushed it carefully away from the edge. As she leaned back in the chair, she lifted her aching feet to the stool and tried hard to catch her breath.

I think I'll nap a bit, she thought and glanced at the clock. It was half-past one. Alvin would be home in a few hours. Maybe sooner. *Please come home sooner*, she thought.

Edna laid on the bed and propped her feet up on a pillow. Napping felt good, and she slept for a few minutes before she woke gasping and coughing. Her breaths were deep as she tried to fill her lungs, but each inhale gurgled in her chest. Edna sat on the edge of the bed and caught her breath. Her throat burned, and every swallow made her fight back the vomit. But sitting up helped her breathing become easier and she relaxed. The baby rolled in her belly, and she felt a kick up under her ribs.

She rubbed her stomach and smiled. "Oh sweetheart. Be easy. You've a way to go before we meet." She pushed herself back to her feet and stood for a moment. She felt a little lightheaded and steadied herself on the doorframe. The sensation passed, and she returned to her tea. The tea was still warm, and she refilled her cup. On a shelf beside the stove was a partial loaf of soda bread wrapped in a cloth. She unwrapped the bread and cut off a piece spreading a little butter and some red currant preserves on it. Alvin preferred the black currants, but red ones were plentiful around the farm, so he learned to like them. As she bit into the bread, she smiled. It reminded her of her mother's bread and the combination of sweet and salty was like heaven in her mouth. She moved to her chair and her little table to resume the blanket. Her feet were already starting to ache again. *I'm asking Alvin to rub my feet when he gets back. It's the least he could do for making me suffer through mutton again*, she thought. She reached for the teacup and found only a blank space. The cup was still on the edge of the stove. She piled the yarn, blanket and knitting needles neatly beside her and stood.

The dizzy sensation returned, and now she felt like she had a bit of a headache. A wave of nausea came over her and she clenched her jaw to fight back the vomit. When it passed, she picked up the cup and brought it to her lips. She sipped a little and felt the hot sting of tears in her eyes. "Oh Alvin, please come home."

Enda turned, carrying her cup and saucer like a precious cargo, so as not to spill it on herself. Her hands were shaking, and the cup rattled against the saucer. She felt a flood of dizziness wash over her head, and she felt as though she was drowning. She wasn't sure if she lost her vision first or heard the cup hit the floor. The room whirled in her mind, and she felt a sadness in her heart to know that her tea set was broken.

Eighteen

Alvin dragged himself back toward the cottage. He wasn't certain how much fence he had mended, but I felt fairly certain the sheep would be safe for a while. He carried a wooden toolbox in one hand and an ax in the other. Most of his fences were stone walls, but the previous tenants had constructed wooden fences to span the sections that were sparse on rocks.

The closer he got to the cottage, the heavier the tools seemed to become. He was dreaming of a steaming hot dish of tea. The spring drizzle had soaked its way to his bones, and he started to wonder if he would ever be able to warm up. The cottage was often cozy, but on stormy days the rain and wind made for stout drafts of air, so his heart sunk a little when he didn't see any smoke rising from the chimney. He arrived back at the barn and piled his tools in the corner. *That's enough work for one day*, he thought and slapped his cap on the door frame to shed the excess water. I hope this dries by morning.

Alvin opened the door and stepped inside, removing his shoes at the door the way Edna liked. He called out as he disrobed. "Did the fire go out darlin'? It's a bit cold. Do you have a pot of tea going?" He stood nearly naked and with his wet clothes piled at his feet.

When she didn't answer, he felt a sudden flood of panic wash over his body. His eye was drawn to the shattered teacup on the floor and in that moment, he felt the hot sting of tears as his heart shattered as well. She was lying on the floor face down and her skin looked bone white.

"Edna!" Alvin dropped to his knees and tried to pick her up. Her skin felt cold and waxy. "Please God. Help us!" he cried aloud as he turned her onto her back and pressed his ear against her chest, listening for the sounds of her heart. He held his breath to fight back the sobs and listened. The silence broke his heart completely, and he wailed. He pulled her to his chest and felt her stomach. There was no movement from the baby, either. Everything they worked for or dreamed of together was gone. Their whole world had been lost in an afternoon.

Alvin held her for an hour or so and just stroked her hair. Blood had flowed from between her legs and her dress was becoming stiff and matted as it dried. Alvin felt utterly alone. *I have to do something*, he thought, but he couldn't bear to leave her. As he sat holding her, Mrs. Duffy came to mind. She had helped deliver many of the babies in the countryside. Maybe she would know what to do.

THE ROBIN'S GAZE

Alvin went to the bedroom and brought a pillow and a blanket from the bed. He lifted Edna's lifeless head and slid the pillow underneath. She looked so peaceful. Like she was sleeping. He gently brushed her hair from her face and had the realization that soon he wouldn't be able to feel her soft hair again. A tear fell from his eye and splashed on her cheek. He wiped it away and ran his forearm across his eyes to stem the tears. "I'm sorry, love. I should have been here."

※ ※ ※ ※

Alvin walked toward the Duffy farm with a lantern dimly guiding his way. He wanted it over with, but dreaded the thought of having to speak to anyone. The mere thought of telling someone she was gone sent tears pouring down his face. The rain seemed to be getting more intense, and, in his mind, it was like the heavens were crying as well at the arrival of such a beautiful soul.

He marched forward in a trance, listening to the splattering of rain and the gentle sucking sound of his own footsteps on the muddy road. He heard a noise to his left and swung the lantern around to see Duffy's bull staring at him over the rock wall. It looked at him with sad eyes, as if it could sense his pain.

Alvin stood at Duffy's door trying to compose himself before he knocked. The more he tried to gather his wits the more he sobbed. He couldn't bring himself to lift his hand to knock. He just stood there with his arms hanging at his sides still gripping his lantern.

The door opened and Angela Duffy stood before him, trying to understand what she was seeing. "Alvin? What's wrong child?"

Alvin looked at Angela and shook his head with tears streaming down his face. He tried to open his mouth, but no words came out, only a sound somewhere between sobbing and gulping.

"Where's Edna? Is she okay?"

Alvin shook his head violently back and forth and finally gulped out the words, "she's gone".

Angela made the sign of the cross and stepped back, pulling Alvin into the house. "Sean! Sean!"

※ ※ ※ ※

Sean had helped Alvin move Edna to the bed and Angela had changed her skirt, then covered her with a blanket from the chest down. Sean had left to tell Alvin's family of the tragedy and to get word to the Collins' in the village.

Angela heated the loaf of soda bread and pulled it from the oven to cool. "Will you take some tea son?"

Alvin sat at the little table and nodded. Angela brought him some tea in the teacup from their wedding. He lifted it to his lips and felt the hot liquid burn his mouth a little. The pain was a welcome sensation to break through the numbness that had set in upon his mind. When he put the cup down, his mind returned to the shattered cup on the floor when he found her, and he pushed the cup away.

"Is it not how you like it?" asked Angela.

"It's fine. I just don't feel like drinking right now."

Angela nodded. She wanted to say something, but somehow, she knew that no matter what she might say, no matter how well intentioned, there was nothing that would be able to ease his pain except time.

Angela sat down beside him and touched his hand. "Alvin. I have to deliver the baby. We can't leave it inside of her."

Alvin felt a catch in his throat, and the tears began flowing again. He simply nodded and wiped his eyes. "I'll help."

"Are you sure, son? I can do it myself if you want."

Alvin took a deep breath and stiffened. "I need to do this."

Angela picked up the wide basin they used for washing and filled it with rags, then poured some water over it. "We'll clean her up and get her dressed before everyone comes."

It was at that moment that the realization came to Alvin that he would have to see Paddy and look him in the eye when he told him his precious jewel was gone. *He'll probably punch me in the face*, he thought. At that moment, Alvin wished that he might, so that he could feel the pain and break his fog of numbness.

Angela removed the blanket and skirt she had placed over Edna. "Help me move her legs. Her body is stiff now and you may have to force it a bit, but it doesn't hurt her. She's feeling no more pain."

"I wish I was feeling no more pain," he croaked.

"Shhh...Hush now. Don't ever wish your life away. She would never want that for you," Angela replied softly.

Alvin stood on the opposite side of the bed and helped force Edna's legs apart. Angela slid her hand inside of Edna to get a hold on the lifeless little body inside of her. Alvin turned his head and closed his eyes to keep from vomiting. The sounds reminded him of cleaning so many animals after slaughter over the years and that seemed to make the nausea even worse.

"It was a wee girl," said Angela.

Alvin turned to see a tiny female body with a large head, and he sobbed. "Was she okay? Her head looks so big."

"She was perfect. The body grows into the head in the last couple of months."

Alvin reached over and touched her tiny, cold hand moving the little fingers with the lightest of touch. He started to laugh a little and cry at the same time. "She was right. She said it was a girl, and it was. She was always right."

"Had you talked about names for the babe?"

Alvin sniffled, "Yes. She liked Nora, and I liked Bridgid."

"Both lovely names."

"We'll call her Nora." As soon as the words left his mouth, he was slapped with the reality that there was no more we. Only him.

Angela cleaned the baby, and Alvin found a shirt and skirt for Edna. He lifted her cold, stiff body and held her while Angela worked the clothes onto her limbs. They hadn't made anything for the baby to sleep in yet, so Alvin pulled a drawer from the dresser and arranged a blanket on the bottom.

Angela tied off the nearly completed Collins blanket and wrapped little Nora, then placed her gently in the drawer.

"Let me reheat your tea now. You need to eat a little something before people start arriving."

Alvin nodded and croaked out the words, "thank you. I don't know how I ever can repay you."

"Someday a friend will need something. Just be there for them and that will be thank you enough."

Nineteen

The rain had finally stopped, and a sliver of sunlight pierced the sky in the distance. I wish that light would fall here, thought Alvin. Every surface of every object was wet, and he was tired of being wet. He loved Ireland, but not today. He longed to be warm and dry with the sunlight on his face. Instead, he had to settle for being envious of people miles away, enjoying a few moments of light.

His family had come, and his mother and sister were preparing food for the other people coming to pay their respects. They still held to the old traditions of keeping a window open so that Edna and Nora's souls might escape the house and fly to heaven, even if it made the room uncommonly dank.

As he stood staring at the lighted hole in the pendulous clouds, he wondered if Edna and Nora were passing through the hole at that moment. He heard the unmistakable sound of a donkey cart creaking and splashing up the road. He turned and saw The Collins clan walking up the path. Paddy walked beside the donkey, followed by Sean and Finn, with Ellen seated in the back.

Alvin stood in the muddy path, frozen in time. He couldn't move and he just stared, waiting to see Paddy's eyes. He imagined them full of anger and rage, but when Paddy's eyes finally met his own, they were like looking into his own. Alvin only saw anguish and pain. As he came closer, Alvin found it harder and harder to breathe. He wanted to wail, but the visceral emotions were gone and now they only seeped slowly out of his heart. It was like the trickling stream that's left, after flood waters have breached a dam.

Paddy handed the lead to Sean and walked to Alvin, still frozen in the road, and wrapped his arm around him and sobbed.

"I'm sorry Paddy," Alvin whispered, through a throat choked with grief.

Paddy squeezed him tighter. "It's not your fault, son."

"I wasn't there ... I was mending fences ... I should have..."

"Nonsense, man. If you were there, the outcome would have been the same. Duffy's wife said that there's no stopping it once it starts." He released Alvin and placed his hands on his hands on Alvin's shoulders. "I know that this was her home, but I'd like to bring her and the child back to the village for the wake and burial."

Alvin seemed to be woken from a fog. He hadn't thought about anything past reuniting her with the families. "Of course you can, Paddy. It would be for the best."

"Thank you, son. It will mean a lot to her mother." Paddy looked back at Sean and Finn, helping her out of the wagon. She moved as though her body had been drained of life. Every movement was slow and required great effort. "She fainted when Duffy told us and struck her head on the table when she fell."

Alvin became immediately concerned. "Is she alright?"

"Her head is fine. It's her heart that needs time to heal. That goes for all of us, I guess."

"It doesn't seem like it will be possible to heal. I don't know what to do."

Paddy turned and patted him on the shoulder. "I don't know how really, but time will heal us. Can you bring me to my daughter now?"

Alvin started for the door with the Collins' lined up behind him. He wanted to say something, but the look of anguish on Ellen's face left him mute and he averted his eyes. The cottage was finally warm again when they entered. Perhaps from the peat stove or perhaps from having so many family members in the house. There was a great comfort in being surrounded by people who loved them.

Friends from the neighboring farms came to pay their respects and offer condolences for the loss. Alvin felt like a child playing the role of a man. He had only been to a handful of wakes and funerals in his whole life, but he mostly remembered the women wailing over the body is what they called keening and the men passing bottles or leaving for the pub for a few pints. They were so far out in the countryside that no one would be at the public house until Edna was returned to the village.

He accepted the well wishes and heartfelt sympathy will all the grace that he could muster.

The worst were the ones that had lost a someone and wanted to explain to him how to feel better. Agnes Fincannon was the worst. She recalled the loss of her husband in a mining accident and how she was able to recover her life after his loss. The man was more than fifty years old, so Alvin found it hard to see the comparison as equal, but then he thought perhaps she just loved him as much as he loved Edna.

The talks weren't helping, and Paddy must have sensed his growing discomfort and broke in to save him. "Agnes, love. Please pardon my intrusion, but I need to see young McGinn here, outside. If I might."

"Oh, my heavens. Of course you can. The men are always needed outside at these types of things," she said with a smile. As Alvin started to rise, she clasped his hand. "Please know that you can stop by anytime to talk. I am always happy for some conversation."

"Thank you, Mrs. Fincannon. I appreciate that."

Alvin stepped outside with Paddy and breathed in the fresh air. Paddy leaned in, "happy for some conversation? It's getting her to shut her gob that's the trick. That woman loves the sound of her own voice."

Alvin actually chuckled a bit. "Thank you, Paddy. The air was getting thick in there."

Paddy reached into his coat pocket and pulled a bottle from the inner pocket and handed it to Alvin. "It's Jamesons."

"I thought you didn't drink?"

"I hardly ever have. But then I never lost my only daughter before. So today I'm having a drink. Maybe the bottle. I don't know. Every person I see has had their hearts broken today. I think I need to escape for a bit."

Alvin uncorked the bottle and brought it to his lips. The whiskey burned his throat as he swallowed, but once he had taken the first drink, the next ones seemed to come easier. "I think I'd like to escape, too."

As the day wore on, the rain returned as a heavy drizzle.

"God damn it," Paddy said, and spat on the ground.

His outburst startled Alvin. "What's wrong?"

"I didn't want my girl and my granddaughter to be soaked by the rain all the way back to the village. But that's the Irish weather for you. Rain, followed by gloom, followed by more rain."

"She'll never know another rainy day. She said she liked the rain because it made everything seem clean," said Alvin.

Paddy forced a smile. "That sounds like her. Always finding good in something."

Alvin passed the bottle back and Paddy pointed up the road. "I believe your friend is coming to pay his respects." It was the coach from Lord Ellingwood's estate and Smith sat hunched under a thick leather Inverness cape and wore a wide-brimmed hat.

When his eyes met Smith's, he could see that Smith's heart was broken as well. It just showed him the power that Edna had to make people feel good and the light that she brought into their lives. He brought the carriage to a stop alongside the collection of donkey carts, and Alvin almost laughed at the absurdity of how it looked. Two massive black horses and an ornate carriage sitting beside four carts and four donkeys that barely reached the carriage team's bellies.

Richard stepped out of the carriage with a splash in the mud, carrying an enormous basket of food. Smith stepped up to take it from him, but Richard waved him away. "Get the drinks from the back and get it to the men here. I'll bring this inside myself."

Smith nodded and headed to the trunk on the back of the wagon.

Richard waddled toward the door and caught Alvin's eye. "I'll pay respects to the mothers first and then I'll be out."

Twenty minutes had passed when Richard emerged from the cottage. His eyes were red rimmed as though he had been crying. He moved toward Alvin and Paddy with a somber countenance and looked them in the eyes.

"My friends I offer you my most heartfelt condolences." Richard turned and pointed to the cottage window where Edna lay on the other side of the glass, to avoid bursting into tears himself. "That girl was perhaps the brightest light I've seen in all of Ireland. I loved her for my friend Alvin the moment my eyes rested upon her. My wife and her sister are away to England, and I can't help think that for all their time spend on beautifying themselves, they could spend the rest of their life at the craft and still only manage to equal the little finger on Edna right hand." He paused and turned back to them. "Her beauty shone outside, but lived here," he thumped the center of his chest with his massive meaty hand. "And the baby girl..." He sniffled as his tears fell and he struggled to produce anymore words.

Alvin stepped forward and patted him on the shoulder. "Thank you, my friend. She loved you as well."

Paddy reached out to shake his hand. "Thank you M'Lord. I appreciate the kindnesses you have done for my daughter and her husband. You arrived just in time or we may have passed each other on the road back to the village."

Richard looked around. "Is there a hearse coming for her?"

"No, we'll bend some branches over my cart and spread a canvas to keep the rain off from them on the way back."

Richard stiffened and felt relief that he set his mind to action. "Nonsense. That woman and that child can ride in my carriage. So will your wife, Mr. Collins. If you'll permit me. I'll ride beside Smith, or maybe I'll walk with my friends."

"That's a generous offer, and we'd be happy to accept your help." He produced the half empty bottle of Jameson from his pocket. "Would you be carin' for a nip?"

Richard took the bottle and pulled the cork. "Is it helping?"

Alvin shrugged, "not yet, but so far it doesn't feel worse."

"That's endorsement enough for me." Richard took a large swallow and nodded his approval. "Oh, that's nice. They can keep their Scotch in London, this is very smooth."

Paddy took the bottle back. "It'll keep us warm for the walk home."

※ ※ ※ ※

Smith pulled the coach to the front of the cottage, and the men used the blankets as a makeshift litter to carry Edna to the carriage and laid her on the seat with Nora swaddled on her chest. Ellen and Annie sat with the bodies, and the parade of donkey carts followed. Richard had instructed Smith to let the horses walk so that Edna and Nora might not be jostled from the seat.

The lamps were lit by the time the procession reached the village. A few people had left early and must have spread the word that they were coming. When the carriage reached the cobblestone, the public houses were emptied and people lined the streets, heads bowed and hats off. This continued throughout the streets and over the hill to the docks and down the lane, right to the Collins' front door.

As they passed, Paddy looked right and left, nodding in acknowledgement to every set of eyes he met. Alvin wondered if he would ever be so respected in his life.

Twenty

It had been two weeks since they had buried Edna and Nora. Alvin sat at the kitchen table, wondering what to do with his life. He knew he should tend to his flock, but he couldn't get out of the chair. He simply sat nibbling on soda bread and cold ham, washing it down with lukewarm tea.

He held the teacup from their wedding and remembered the shattered cup on the floor beside Edna. The image in his head made him cry all over again. He picked up the cup and walked to the door, flinging it open wide. He cocked his arm behind his head about to throw the cup when he heard his mother's voice. "That's not what Edna would have wanted."

Alvin stopped and turned to the voice. His mother and father were walking up the road with the donkey cart. Jameson walked behind them, and Emma sat in the back, holding a black and white, furry object. His heart dropped at the sight of a dog.

He lowered the cup. "Is that Emily's dog?"

Jameson ran up the road ahead of Ambrose and Annie. "We brought it for you, to help tend the sheep."

"I don't want it, and I don't need it. Now I'll have to feed the God damned thing."

A flash of anger crossed Annie's face. "Alvin! Don't blaspheme. We know you're hurting, but don't take the lord's name in vain. What would Edna say?"

"What would she say? How would I know? Ask God, he's the one that took her from me and my sweet girl too! Ask him! ... Wait, let me!'" Alvin placed the teacup on a stool beside the door and cupped his hand around his mouth. "Lord! Can you ask Edna what she'd say?!" He moved his cupped hand to his ear and listened to the right, then swapped hands and listened to the left. "Nothing to say?! I thought so." Then he turned and glared at his mother.

Jameson and Emma stared in disbelief. No one ever spoke to Annie that way without getting the back of a hand across the mouth or a wooden spoon across their ass. Annie glared right back and took a step toward Alvin when Ambrose grabbed her by the elbow.

"Give us a minute, love."

Ambrose walked to Alvin. "Come over here and talk to me, son." He took Alvin by the elbow and guided him around the corner of the cottage out of sight from the others. He turned and face Alvin with sad eyes. "Now listen, son..." Ambrose slugged Alvin in the stomach, knocking the wind out of him. Alvin looked up in shock and his face turned red as he struggled to take a breath. Ambrose reached his arm across his body and recoiled with the back of his hand across Alvin's mouth, knocking him to the ground. Before Alvin knew what was happening, Ambrose had him by the hair and pulled him to his feet and dunked his head in the rain barrel. When he took another breath, he dunked it again, then pulled Alvin from the barrel and pushed him to the ground.

"Are you awake now, son? Because you must have been sleepwalkin' or dreamin' with your eyes open if you thought you'd speak to your mother like that. Either that or maybe you've lost all of your good sense. Which is it? Sleepwalking or you've lost your fucking faculties?"

Alvin gasped and coughed as he regained his ability to breathe. "I'm sorry Da. I'm hurting... In my heart."

"We know that, Alvin. We came to bring you comfort, not listen to you curse God and berate your mother. You need to get a fucking hold of yourself."

"I can't move forward. I feel lost."

Ambrose reached out a hand. Alvin looked at it for a long moment then grabbed him and stood. "People die son. I'll die. Your ma will die. People you know, people you love. They'll all die someday, but I can assure you of one thing I know to be true."

Alvin wiped a little blood from his split lip. "What's that?"

"They don't want you there with them. They want you to live your life. Edna included. A day will come when you'll see her on the other side. But it won't be anytime soon."

Alvin nodded and pushed the wet hair from his face. "I'm not sure how to go on."

"Your best start would be to go to the front and apologize to your mother. From there...just try to accomplish something each day. If you set your mind to tasks, it'll keep your thoughts occupied with something other than your losses."

"I will Da. And I'm sorry for my blasphemy."

Ambrose chuckled. "I don't give a good God damn about blasphemy, but your mother does, so tell her you're sorry."

When Alvin walked around the corner of the cottage, he found Emma and Jameson trying to teach the dog to fetch a stick. Emma would throw it, and Jameson would run to it and pretend to put it in his mouth. "See ... like this ... dog." The dog sat looking at Emma and then Jameson, but never offered to move. When it finally grew bored with watching them chase the stick, he laid down on the road and closed his eyes.

"I hope it manages sheep better than fetching," said Alvin.

"I wouldn't count on it. But I suspect it can find your table scraps easily enough. I've seen that dog in the village a time or two lurking about the pubs," replied Ambrose.

"I really don't want a dog."

"I say you do, so take it or we can slip back around the corner for another go."

"Okay," Alvin replied with a frown.

"Tell them you love it. They wanted to do something good for you and they spent hours trying to catch the damned thing."

"If I'm lucky maybe it will run away." Alvin walked over and gave two sharp whistles, and the dog jumped to its feet. He whistled twice again and slapped his thigh, and the dog came running to him. Alvin patted his head and tugged at his ear. "Good boy." Emma and Jameson stood with broad smiles and a look of pride that they had done something good.

"Do you like it?' asked Emma.

"I do. What's its name?"

Jameson frowned. "Kellen said you should call it Eejit, because it's so dumb."

"Oh really? Well, I think I'm going to name it Kellen then. Kelly for short."

Emma and Jameson laughed and hopped around. "Yes, yes. Call it Kellen. That will be so funny."

Ambrose shook his head. "It's obvious the dog's not very bright, so the name fits to be sure."

"What name is that?" asked Annie from the doorway, standing with her arms folded.

"The dog is named Kellen," Ambrose said with a grin.

"I don't know if I care for that," she replied with a frown.

"It's just in fun Ma," said Alvin.

"I realized that, but what did that dog ever do to you?"

Everyone erupted in laughter. Alvin took his mother's hands. "I'm sorry Ma. I wasn't myself and I acted like a proper jackass."

"We all miss her, son. Let's try to get through this together."

"Okay." He hugged her and she squeezed him tight.

"What's wrong with the teacup? It doesn't look cracked," said Annie.

Alvin looked at the cup on the table. It looked delicate and pristine, just like Edna. "She loved those cups and when I found her, one was broken on the floor beside her. So now it's a set for three, not four and looking at it reminds me of her."

"Is that bad? To see something beautiful and think of her."

"It makes me miss her," he said in a soft voice choking back tears.

"Instead of thinking about how much you miss her, try to think about how much she loved the tea set and how it is beautiful like she was. Set your mind to the good things about her, not the fact that she's gone."

"Thank you, Ma. I'll try."

Annie smiled. "Perhaps I should place these back in the wood case they came I and then when you are ready, you can take them out again."

"I think I'd like that."

After they had left, Alvin sat in the kitchen and watched the dog sleeping on the floor. "I think you look about as ambitious as I feel, boyo." He went to the stove and tore bits of ham from the bone, cut a slice of bread and wrapped them in a cloth. "Let's tend the flock and see what you know."

THE ROBIN'S GAZE

At the sound of two quick whistles, Kelly lifted his head and stared at Alvin.

"Well, let's go." Alvin held a morsel of ham out and the dog came over and sat in front of Alvin looking desperate. A small stream of saliva ran from its mouth and dripped onto the floor. Alvin tossed the bit of meat, and the dog snapped it out of the air. "I guess they should have thrown ham instead of a stick. Let's go."

Alvin opened the gate and Kelly sprinted into the meadow toward the small flock. The sheep clustered together quickly, and Kelly started driving them toward the cottage.

That is amazing, h*e must do it by instinct,* thought Alvin.

As he watched Kelly race back and forth around the herd, he realized that this dog had been trained by someone. Someone who was probably missing a dog for their herd right now. "Oh well, he's a stray, so finders' keepers, losers' weepers," he said aloud.

He walked to the rock wall and lifted a large flat stone. Underneath it was a brown bottle. He lifted the bottle and pulled the cork with his teeth and spat the cork into his hand. The whiskey smelled strong, and he braced himself. He wasn't a big drinker, but he was acquiring a taste for it. The liquor burned his throat, and he took a breath. Once his eyes cleared, he took another long drink.

He looked at the half empty bottle and laid it back in its hiding place. Alvin was about to replace the flat rock when he changed his mind and put the bottle in his pocket, sat down beside the rock wall and drank some more of the whiskey, watching the dog herd his flock.

The sun was setting, and his pants felt damp from the grass. He wobbled a bit when he stood and then whistled loudly, and Kelly came running. "Good boy. Let's go back inside." His first couple of steps took him by surprise. "So, this is what it's like to be drunk."

Twenty-One

Alvin woke to the smell of dog breath in his nostrils. His body ached and his head was pounding. He cracked one eye open and realized that he was sleeping on the floor and Kelly was curled up against him.

"Christ. What a stink." He pushed Kelly away and got to his hands and knees. When he stood, the room seemed to sway a little, and then he regained his balance. He felt shaky and his mouth felt like it had been stuffed with wool all night. He saw the brown bottle on the floor and picked it up. A little whiskey remained, and he looked around for the cork. After a cursory look, he stopped and drank the rest of the whiskey.

He looked at the stove and considered making a fire, but drank yesterday's cold tea instead. His stomach churned and acid burned his throat. Alvin cut a large slice of bread and slathered it in butter. He chewed it in big bites and the bread started to make his insides feel better almost immediately.

The tea settled his stomach as well, and he sat back to contemplate the day. Now that he had something to eat he looked around for something to give the dog. He was going to save the ham bones for making a soup, but decided it wouldn't be worth trying to save them for something he'd likely never get around to making. Alvin laid the ball of meat and bone on the table and split it with a rough knife.

"Half today and half tomorrow. After that, we'll figure something else out," he said and tossed a piece to Kelly. The dog sniffed it and plopped down with the joint between his paws and gnawed at it with a grinding sound of tooth on bone.

Alvin stepped outside to use the loo and, as the cool air hit him, he felt a little more awake. Perhaps I'll work on that fence today, he thought and looked around. He had no neighbors, and no one was on the road, so he relieved himself on the grass at the side of the cottage door. He chuckled that it was something he would have never done if Edna was around, and then immediately felt ashamed that he was pissing beside his own door. *What kind of man would do that?* He thought. He looked at the sky. "Sorry love."

Alvin went to the fence and opened the gate for the sheep to come out. They filed out and made their way across the field to graze. Once they were all out of the barn, he stepped in to shovel dung onto the heap. The smell was making his stomach churn again, and he stepped back into the cool air. Alvin rested on the dung fork and looked at the wooden boxes stacked in the back of the barn. He moved the top two and took a brown ceramic jug from the wooden box and pulled the cork. It was hard cider from the fall. Alvin took a drink and nodded with approval. The gallon jug was much too cumbersome to lug around all day, so he grabbed a quart jar that held some nails and poured them into a small wooden box, then took the jar to the rain barrel for rinsing. Rust from the nails still stained the bottom of the jar, but he figured a little rust never hurt anyone, and filled the jar with cider.

By the time he had cleaned the barn and moved the dung to the heap, he had finished his cider. He filled the jar again and went into the cottage. He opened the crock of salted mutton and pulled a small slab, and placed it in a kettle. *I wonder if it's safe to feed dogs sheep*, he thought. Seems like they'd gain a taste for it. Then it would be like a fox guarding the henhouse.

Alvin opened a jar of carrots and poured them in with the mutton. He started a fire and sipped his cider while he waited for it to cook. The smell was turning his stomach a bit. Prior to this, he had little experience cooking and felt like he must be making a mistake. He moved the kettle to the edge of the heat to let it simmer for a while.

He didn't care much for the smell at all. When his mother cooked, she always used spices, so Alvin looked at what they had and started adding a few. First, he added rosemary. He had always liked the smell of that. Then he threw a little thyme and sage into the pot. The smell had already become more appetizing. He used a wooden spoon to have a taste. The broth was so salty it made him gulp his cider. The only water he had in the house was the cold tea and he couldn't see how that would be appetizing. Rather than go outside to fetch more water, he poured some of his cider into the mix. It had a faint vinegar smell, but it was still edible. He drained the rest of his cider and removed the pot from the heat while he refilled his jar. He brought the pitcher they used for water and filled that at the same time.

When he returned, he stabbed the single hunk of meat with a fork and spooned some carrots over it and sat down at the table. I should have cut it up, he thought. Ma always cut it up. He sawed at the meat and started chewing. It was tough. Like chewing leather. Then he remembered that his mother cooked salted meat for a very long time. Hours, in fact. The saltiness of the meal was making him thirsty, and he drank the cider in big gulps.

When he finished the carrots, he tried again to eat the meat, but between the salt and the toughness, it didn't seem worth it. So, he pitched the mutton to Kelly who sniffed at it and didn't bother to even try it.

"You may regret that. You'll be good and hungry before you get a chance to eat again." Alvin stood and balanced himself on the table. He looked at Kelly and laughed. "Is it me, or is the room a bit off kilter?"

Hanging on a hook near the door was a large leather bladder he used for water when he worked his land. It'll hold cider, just as well as water, he thought and pulled the skin from its hook.

He opened the door and whistled twice. Kelly jumped to his feet and followed close behind him.

When he got to the jug of cider, he realized it was half empty, he thought to himself, *damn it. I need to find me some more of this*. He filled the skin and loaded a hammer, nails and a saw into his toolbox, and started across the field. "Come on dog!"

Kelly ran up the hill and waited patiently, for Alvin as he trudged along with his tools. When he reached the top, he sat down at the base of a tree and pulled the stopper from the skin. Alvin took a drink and waited a few moments before taking another.

Alvin leaned his back against the tree and looked out at the cloudy horizon. "Edna. I don't know what to do with myself. I miss you so terribly." He took another drink and then another. "Is the baby, okay? I wish we could have held her together. I'd give anything to hold you again." He searched the sky as if she might present herself one last time. But of course, she never did and continued to drink. When the skin was empty, he closed his eyes and slept a bit. He was startled awake by the sound of Kelly barking at something. Alvin opened one eye and saw a figure coming across the field.

For a moment, he felt excited, thinking it was Edna. His excitement shifted to panic upon realizing it was her father Paddy, who had come for a visit.

He stood up quick and staggered then grabbed the tree to prevent from falling over.

Paddy didn't look very happy to see Alvin.

"Young McGinn. Been at the spirits I see."

"Just a wee bit of cider left over from the wake."

Paddy scowled. "The house is a damned mess. There's a stinking stew in the kettle and the doorway smells like piss. Are you going to let the sheep out to roam next? The gate was open, and you were asleep. They could be halfway across county Kerry by now if they weren't so dense." Paddy picked up the skin and sniffed, then crinkled his nose. "What ails you, boy?"

Alvin looked at the ground and started sobbing. "I miss her terribly."

Paddy slapped him across the face, and Alvin rubbed his hand lightly over his burning skin. Paddy pointed a bony finger in Alvin's face. "You want to be a man. Start acting like one. Do you think you are the only one that misses her? She was the sunlight in my life for seventeen years. Now I only see darkness. But I go on. It's time you do too."

Alvin looked Paddy in the eye. "I don't know how."

Twenty-Two

Paddy surveyed the state of the cottage and sighed. "Can you make a proper pot of tea, son? I already know you can't make a stew."

"Yes, of course. I'll make some now." Alvin opened the stove and slid another turve of peat onto the dwindling fire and blew on it. The embers glowed, and the peat belched a small column of thick smoke before bursting into flame. Alvin shut the door and slid the kettle from earlier to the far edge of the stove and clapped a cover on it. Paddy was right. It stank.

Paddy sat at the table and pulled a clay pipe from his pocket and rooted around in the tobacco with the end of a matchstick. "Sit."

Alvin sat opposite him and watched as he struck the match and drew three big puffs on the pipe. Paddy said nothing for a long time. He just studied Alvin. The look was not anger or pity. It was something akin to looking into his soul.

"So." Alvin jumped at the break in silence. "You've turned to drink to solve your woes?"

Alvin looked at the floor. "I don't know what I'm doing." He had never been a drinker, and he hated how he felt when he woke up, but the pain of being awake seemed more than he could bear. Paddy put his pipe on the table and stroked at his stubble. "Do you know Michael McNally from the village?"

"I don't think so," replied Alvin.

"Mike is an old friend of mine, and he came to see me yesterday at the boat." He picked his pipe back up and puffed it again. "I grew up with Mike's sons. They were fishermen like me. One day back in 1880, I was out fishing. I was having a poor day in terms of the catch, and I could see a bank of dark clouds as big as a mountain rolling toward me, so I weighed anchor and got back to the dock without a moment to lose. I moored the boat; it was a smaller boat than I have now, and I raced to get her unloaded ahead of the weather. When I got the last of my catch off the boat, I saw Mike looking at the empty slip where his son's moored. He'd asked if I had seen them and I hadn't since the early morning when they were loading gear." He drew on the pipe and blew the smoke up into the air. "They never came home. We found parts of their boat washed up on the shore two days later, but they were gone."

"Jesus. Is that why he came to see you?"

Paddy nodded. "He said the only advice I can give you is this. You're not the same, you never will be, so stop trying to go back. The sooner you realize this, the sooner you move forward."

"It's only been a couple weeks," Alvin said in protest.

"I don't think he was meaning to say, move on today. I took his meaning to be you won't heal until you can let go."

Alvin decided that whether or not he believed it, it was probably best to agree, rather than debate. "I see his point. I just can't move my mind to anything else except Edna. I'm afraid if I don't think about her every day, I may forget what she looked like."

Paddy chuckled, "I have the same fears." He tried to reignite his pipe, but it had extinguished. He placed it on the table. "I know you're hurting, but drink is not the answer. It's something that sneaks up on you and then it has you. You'll only live, to drink."

"But that's after years, right?"

"I don't know how long it takes. It's different for each man. But I am certain that no matter how many spirits you pour down your gullet, you'll never fill that hole." Paddy leaned forward and tapped Alvin's chest with his finger. "It fills itself in, over time. There's no other cure for it."

The water on the stove was starting to boil and Alvin made the tea the way Edna had showed him.

Paddy took his cup and sipped it. "Well, you can make a proper pot of tea, I'll give you that."

"That's one thing, I guess. I'm not too certain about much else. Farming is a bit of a mystery to me. McGinns have always been laborers, so I don't mind the work. I'm just never sure what I am supposed to be doing each day."

Paddy shook his head. "I'm afraid I'd be little help to you there. I've never so much as planted a potato. Now I can tell you anything about a fish you'd be caring to know, but you may have to ask your neighbors for help with what the hell a sheep is thinking."

Alvin pointed at Kelly. "The god damned dog knows more about it than I do."

Paddy looked at the dog as if he was trying to recollect where he knew it from. "Where'd you get the dog from?"

"My younger sister and brother claimed it was a stray and brought it here. I really didn't want a dog, but this one seems pretty bright, so I'll probably keep it."

Paddy's expression flattened. "I don't think that dog is a stray."

"My father said he'd seen roaming around the pubs in the village."

"It probably was. His owner is a terrible drinker named Carrigan. Bruce Carrigan. He's a sheep farmer too, on the other side of the village. He is often passed out somewhere along the way to his farm, so he probably thinks it ran off. It roams the pubs looking for scraps. Carrigan's been looking for it around the docks."

Alvin's heart sunk. "Are you certain?"

"I am son. I've seen this dog with him half a hundred times. His name is Nero."

The mention of his name caused Kelly to whip his head around, his eyes scanning for something.

"God dammit. I knew I didn't want a dog and as soon as I like it a bit, it's gone."

Paddy patted him on the arm. "I'm sorry, son. Carrigan is a miserable, drunken son of a whore, but that is his dog."

"I'll bring him to the village tomorrow. Do you know where this Carrigan lives?"

"He's just outside of the village. First farm past the train station."

"Okay. I'll bring him first light."

Paddy nodded. "That's a good idea. If you bring him after lunchtime, check O'Malley's first. He's likely to be passed out in a corner there." Paddy stood to leave and stopped. he turned to look at Alvin. "Go early and when you're done, come see me and I'll take you out on the boat for a bit. It's quite peaceful."

Alvin felt excited at the prospect of going onto paddy's boat. "I will. I'll come as soon as I'm done."

Paddy grinned. "Good. See you then and have something in your stomach other than liquor, or you'll likely regret it."

Alvin walked to the village, with Kelly bounding along by his side. He genuinely liked the dog, and that was unexpected. The only pet they ever had was a large orange cat named Festus who kept the house free of mice. The cat had a surly disposition and had a habit of glaring at anyone walking by. If you made the mistake of coming too close, you risked being rewarded with a flashing stroke across a hand or forearm. It was strictly off-limits to petting, cuddling, or waking. The thing about Festus was that he had four sets of double claws, which left twice the wound of a typical cat. Festus lived to be somewhere around seventeen years old, and they were all so happy to be free of his menace that no one ever suggested another cat.

The sun was breaking through the fog and the walk felt almost pleasant. He wasn't certain what type of reception to expect. Maybe Carrigan would give him a reward. Somehow, he doubted that. He was thinking about how to buy the dog, but he had no money until he could sell some wool again.

When he entered the village, Kelly sniffed around the public houses, looking for any refuse. "I should have found something for you to eat," Alvin said, a little embarrassed that he didn't even have food fit for a dog.

They passed the train station, and Kelly stopped. "Hey let's go!" Alvin whistled and slapped his thigh twice. Kelly dropped his head and tail and sauntered along as if he were sensing the inevitable. Alvin wasn't sure who looked more downcast, him or the dog.

When he reached the Carrigan farm, he knew it right away. It looked like a place that hadn't been cared for in years. It was like looking at the future of his farm if he were a drunk his whole life. The yard was overgrown, and the loo could be smelled from ten yards away. He took a deep breath and knocked on the door.

There was no answer, so he knocked louder. *Maybe he's not here*, thought Alvin. *Or maybe he died from filth.* He was about to leave when the door to the loo swung open and a small, wrinkled man with pale blue eyes and no teeth emerged.

"There you are Nero, you mangy eyed devil! Come!"

Kelly walked at a slow pace and sat before his master. Carrigan glared at the dog and pointed to the field. "Go!" Kelly ran into the field where a large flock of sheep were scattered, and he wasn't Kelly and more. He was Nero again.

"Where'd you find him? I went into O'Malley's place and when I came out he was gone."

"I didn't, my younger brother and sister found it wandering and brought it to my farm. They thought it was a stray."

Carrigan gave him a skeptical look and then smiled. "Oh well, it's not the first time. He's been away to half a dozen other farms over the years."

Alvin really didn't have anything to say. He was disappointed but it was Carrigan's dog.

"Well, if he shows up again. I'll know where to bring him."

Carrigan grinned through a wide mouth of toothless gums, "Stop by O'Malley's sometime and I'll but you a pint."

"I'm not really much of a drinker."

Carrigan had a loud, raspy laugh. "Well, you can buy me one then!"

Twenty-Three

Alvin hurried to the docks as soon as he was done at Carrigan's. He never wanted a dog, but he missed Kelly already. There was something comforting about it to him. The dog seemed to know his owner's pain and stayed near, offering comfort. Maybe that was the point of keeping a pet and the relationship benefitted both parties.

Paddy was loading gear on to the Ellen Marie when he caught sight of Alvin. "McGinn, come lend a hand here. We'll shove off once we get this gear loaded. I'll jump aboard you hand me those crates."

Alvin quickened his pace and handed Paddy the heavy wooden boxes. "What's in these?"

"Cordage in some and spare sails in the others. I bought these from a boat a few slips down from a fella who thought he'd get in on the fishing game, but learned it's harder than it looks. Fishing is not for everyone."

"Have you ever had to change a sail at sea?" asked Alvin.

"Twice. But never on this boat. I learned to fish on Ellen's father Tom Ryan's boat, the Mary Grace. It was an old Galway Hooker like this one. It was a Bad Mor and was a forty-four foot long boat. Oh how she griped in a blow. I'd bale the old bitch as fast as I could, and you could watch the water seep through the seams when she heeled over. Tom would yell out. Bale or swim Collins it's a long way to shore! Then cackle like a mad man."

Alvin climbed aboard and looked around. The deck was meticulously clean except for the gear they had just loaded. "Does this boat leak?"

Paddy laughed. "Only over the sides in a swell. But I stay in on days like that. This is a Hooker too, called a Pucan. It's twenty-eight feet. I could have a bigger boat, but this one handles well and takes fewer men to handle."

"Where is Tom's boat now?"

Paddy pulled his pipe from his pocket and pointed out to sea. "In the North Atlantic. He was a terrible drinker and tempted fate one too many times. Some boats said they saw him dis-masted and tossing in the sea." Paddy loaded the pipe while he talked. "He had a local lad with him he had picked up in the pub. He liked to pay men in whiskey and tobacco when he could. The boy was named Walsh, and he was a local half-wit who had been knocked about by a horse and had his skull broken. He lived, but he was more animal than man. Tom fed him cheap whiskey and gave him a few shillings each night." Paddy lit his pipe. "Tom was out with this Walsh, and they were bobbing about like an apple in a stream. The other boats could see the squall coming at them and tried everything to tack and get them a lifeline. But It was too much of a blow and the squall rolled over the Mary Grace like a thick black carpet. The boats maneuvered best they could to manage the squall themselves and when it passed, they looked back, and the Mary Grace was gone. They found a few boxes floating and part of her mast that had snapped off. But nothing else."

Alvin stood in stunned silence. He could see the pain on Paddy's face as he thought about his father-in-law. "That must have been hard on everyone."

"It was." He puffed his pipe and exhaled. "Ellen's mother came to live with us until she passed a few years back. She and Edna shared a room. They were very close. For my part, I vowed never to allow liquor on my boat ever and I stay away from it myself. Tom spent his whole life on the water and still he was lost. If he had been sober with a reliable crew, he'd probably still be here today."

"Edna never told me that story."

"Well, she didn't know the details. According to her grandmother, Tom was a Saint who helped the needy and never missed mass. I can assure you he missed all the services, unless they were being held at O'Malley's," he said with a chuckle. "I already unmoored up front, just pick up that pole in the hooks along the side and fend us off so we don't scrape the paint any more than it is already."

❀ ❦ ❀ ❦

They sailed along a channel into the open sea, and Alvin liked the motion of the boat. Every time it rose and fell, a light spray would hit his face, and he could taste the salty water on his lips. He looked back to see the rugged cliffs that served as a barrier between the earth and sea. Gulls circled the cliffs looking for crabs or other unsuspecting prey along the beach to be snatched up and dropped onto the rocks to become their next meal.

"Are we going to fish?" asked Alvin.

"No. I don't think so, son. Let's just ride along and enjoy the day."

Alvin nodded and looked out to sea. It was peaceful, and he could see why it appealed to so many men.

Paddy opened a metal box and placed it between them. It was filled with cold meat, cheese, and bread. "Help yourself. It's all good solid food and that will help to keep things down, but you look like you're doing alright."

"I feel good," replied Alvin. He looked around, trying to get his bearings as to their direction. "Are we traveling west?"

Paddy glanced at the compass beside him. "A bit North of West."

"If we kept traveling on this course, would we end up in America?"

"Greenland would be more likely." Paddy studied the sails and was satisfied with the amount of wind they drew. "If we sailed due west we'd end up in Canada. South of west and we'd find America. Ireland sits in a higher latitude than the United States."

They sailed on and Alvin closed his eyes and turned his face to the sun. It felt good as his face warmed.

"Have you ever thought about going there?" Paddy asked.

Alvin opened his eyes and looked around. There was nothing but the sea ahead of them. "Going where?"

"America. Or Canada. A lot of Irish have moved there. I hear different stories about what happens over there, but they don't ever seem to come back, so it can't be all bad."

Alvin had never really considered it. He thought he would always live in Ireland. He liked reading about places in books and imagined visiting tropical islands and big cities, but he never imagined himself living in any of those places. He figured these would be adventures to come back and tell everyone in the village about. "I don't know what I'd do there. I doubt they burn peat and I'm a middling farmer at best."

Paddy laughed. "They have so much work there, that they can't find enough people to do it. They used to have slaves to their work, but now they need free men to do it."

Alvin scratched his head and contemplated explaining to Paddy how he had it all wrong, but he decided to let him think what he wanted. There would be less chance of offending him that way.

"I'm sure they do. It's a big country and they keep moving west."

"I think you should consider it at least. You could sell your farm and probably have enough to start a new one there."

Alvin considered that for a minute. "Perhaps. Although I have no knowledge of how much land costs there."

Paddy scratched at his stubble. "I don't know either. But I suppose that like most places it runs the gamut from high to low. If it's as big as you say it is, farmland is probably reasonably priced. You should ask your friend Richard the next time he's back. I'm sure he knows all about those things. Rich men usually do." Paddy looked up at the sky, "I think we've traveled west long enough. It's time to turn back." As Paddy moved the rudder, the vessel swung around as gracefully as a ballerina on the swells and the sails shifted their wind from one side to the other.

Now the breeze was on Alvin's back and he turned up his collar to keep the breeze from making his neck too cold. He sat looking forward, but now his mind was in America. He tried to recall what Arthur McCall looked like. He remembered how close he was to Ambrose, when he was a child, but he couldn't bring his image to the front of his mind except that he was a large man with red hair and a booming voice. Perhaps writing to Arthur would be the place to start his journey. Maybe Kellen would be interested as well. He'd feel safer going with someone he could rely upon.

Twenty-Four

Alvin walked each day after chores to avoid being around the cottage. In his mind, he could see it looming behind him. Empty, lifeless and filled with memories of all he had lost. He entered the village as morning mass had ended, and the streets were bustling with parishioners rushing to work, and widows clustered in cliques at the foot of the church steps.

Alvin saw his bench clear and being watched over by his old friend the hooded crow. It eyed each passer-by with a cool weariness. Although the bird was far too high to be pestered, it still watched as if the throng below were a parcel of interlopers. Alvin reached into his pocket for a crust of bread, but he had eaten it all. He had nothing for the bird.

Alvin sat and looked at the crow with a recollection that brought him back to the day he waited for Edna on that very spot. It was a time when anything seemed possible and every thought was forward to the life they'd make together. Now his mind drifted to the realization that none of the plans he had made in his mind would be coming true and he couldn't shake the image of Tom Ryan's dismasted boat bobbing helplessly under the coming storm.

When the people had cleared away, he saw Father Flynn standing at the top of the steps, watching him. He gave Alvin a kindly look and walked over to the bench. "Young McGinn. You missed mass."

"I'm sorry Father. I was walking."

Father Flynn nodded in understanding. "Walking is good for the mind... How are you holding up, son?"

Alvin hated that question, but Father Flynn was just doing his job, so he didn't react with anger.

"Not well, I'm afraid. I miss her terribly." Alvin felt a hot tear roll down his cheek. "I'm wondering if I offended God somehow to cause him to take her from me."

Father Flynn put a hand on Alvin's shoulder. "God doesn't punish us. He loves us."

"I feel like he's forsaken me."

Two busybody widows passed by the bench, "Have a lovely day, Father." The closest one said, and Father Flynn gave a curt "thank you."

Father Flynn sighed. "Would you like to speak inside?"

Alvin looked up with red-rimmed eyes. "I don't need to give confession, Father."

"Not confession, just some privacy."

Alvin looked at the doors to the church, and he recalled the last time he had seen them. His brothers and Edna's brothers, along with some fisherman friends of Paddy were carrying her casket from the church to the graveyard.

"I'm content to stay here I think," he replied.

Father Flynn turned and faced Alvin. "That's fine. Some people will disagree with me, but I will tell you what I believe about death."

Alvin wiped his eyes and straightened up to show he was listening.

"God doesn't punish us. He loves us. He keeps his kingdom open for us for when we die. But God doesn't take our loved ones, and the devil doesn't kill them. We are all fragile and our end can come at any time. So, we prepare our souls so that we are ready for our time."

"I think I feel like I did something, because I need it to make sense... Why she died."

Father Flynn shrugged. "I don't know why. But she was a pure and loving girl. She is certainly with the lord now."

Alvin dropped his eyes to the ground. "I want to believe it's true."

"Search your heart. Could she and your daughter be anywhere else?"

Alvin thought about it and felt a sliver of relief in his heart. Father Flynn was right. Edna was the kindest person he had ever known. She could only be in heaven.

"No. She can only be there. Thank you, Father."

Caw!

Father Flynn pointed up. "You see Francis agrees."

"The crow is named Francis?"

"Well, I named him Francis after Saint Francis of Assisi. He was here living in this tree when I came to this parish. Nearly seven years now. He's remarkable. He's lived well beyond the average crow."

"I have fed him bread before," Alvin said with a smile.

Father Flynn folded his hands in his lap and watched Francis. "Soda bread is his favorite. Perhaps that's the key to his long life."

"Thank you, Father. Your words helped more than you know."

"You're welcome, Alvin and remember this. God loves us even when we don't love ourselves. So don't turn your back on him."

"I won't, Father." Alvin stood to leave and stopped. "Father, do you believe in the superstition that your loved ones can watch you from heaven, through the eyes of a robin?"

Father Flynn stopped and smiled. "I do." He placed his hand on Alvin's shoulder. "We have no way of knowing all of God's mysteries, so that seems just as plausible as anything else."

"Thank you, Father."

※ ※ ※ ※

Alvin stopped at his childhood home on his way back to the cottage. Ambrose sat on a stump looking at the door to the home. He tilted his head a little and then tilted it to the other side.

"Something wrong?" Alvin asked, and Ambrose jumped a little at the sound of his voice. He had been so deep in thought, he never heard Alvin approach.

"The doorframe's out of square and now the door won't shut right." Ambrose stroked the stubble on his chin. "I'll need to find some wood to make some shims. But that's a project for later. What brings you around."

"Just walking,"

Ambrose looked around. "Where's the dog?"

"I had to bring the dog back to its rightful owner."

"Who might that be?"

"Bruce Carrigan."

Ambrose spat on the ground. "For the love of Christ, that old drunk doesn't deserve a dog like that. The damn dog is smarter than he is."

Alvin laughed. "The dog wasn't too happy about going back. It moped from the station to Carrigan's."

"Well, get a new dog. You can train it. Most of those collies are born with a gift for herding. Wouldn't take a lot of training to make a serviceable dog for your place."

Alvin hung his head. "I don't know that I want that place anymore. Or to be a sheep farmer."

Ambrose studied Alvin. "Don't be rash, son. I know that you are hurting, but everything you ever saved is tied up there."

Alvin looked up with eyes watery. "And everything I ever wanted in life died there. I don't like to have a meal, or even sleep there. Too many memories." He wiped his eyes. "Two nights ago, I sat for an hour staring at the beam I fell from when we were rebuilding the roof. My only thought was that if I had broken my neck, I'd be free of the pain I'm feeling now."

"Alvin. Don't talk like that. Taking one's own life is a sin."

"I wouldn't do that. I just can't see my way forward living at that cottage, so I was thinking of selling and moving into the village."

Ambrose frowned. "And do what, exactly? There's not enough work now. If you work as a field hand, you'll make next to nothing, and you might as well have stayed at your own place. There are too many fishermen as well."

"I couldn't do that. Every fish I caught would remind me of her. Paddy suggested I go to America."

Ambrose scratched his head. "Arthur McCall's there."

"I thought of him, but I'm not sure what I'd do there."

"Start a new life in the new world. Many Irishmen made a new start there."

Alvin shrugged. "I'm having a hard time to see a way forward."

Ambrose shook his head in frustration. "For Christ's sake Alvin. You say you can't live in the cottage. I don't want you to move back here. Sometimes people need to move on. It's not running away from your troubles. I want you to start a new life there." He paused and nodded. "And take Kellen with you. There's nothing here for you two. In fact, maybe Jameson should go as well. He's twelve now, he could have a good life over there. You all could."

Alvin thought for a long moment. Together, they would at least have each other to rely upon. He hadn't seen Arthur McCall in over ten years. Maybe he wouldn't want company, he thought. "What will Ma say? And what about Emily?"

"Your mother won't be happy at first, but she wants the best for you all, so I'll bring her around. As for your sister. I don't think your mother would survive without her here. She may not want to let Jameson go, but there are troubles brewing here and she doesn't want any of you mixed up in it."

"Kellen will want to stay and fight if it comes to a war," said Alvin.

Ambrose sighed. "I expect all the men will. But if you are in America, you won't be a part of it. Hell, you'll probably never hear tell of it."

"Can I think on it a bit?"

Ambrose chuckled. "Of course. It would take some time to plan things. Let me send a letter to Arthur and see what opportunities there are. I'd hate to send you there to discover there's no work."

"I have to go tend my flock and milk. I'll think about it for a few days and decide."

Alvin started down the road and resumed his walk to the cottage. The idea of moving to America both intrigued and terrified him at the same time. He had heard some fishermen talking about Canada and said that there were so many trees, you could never count them in a lifetime. Alvin looked around and saw fields and hedgerows, but only the occasional tree. *I could probably count the trees here before lunchtime*, he thought. *Maybe I'll ask Richard what he knows about America.*

Twenty-Five

It took several weeks for Ambrose's letter to reach Arthur McCall and several weeks more for his letter to return to Ireland. The letter was filled with stories about America and life in Maine and why Ambrose and Annie should come with the boys, but the general message was that any of the McGinns were always welcome.

Arthur had settled his family in the town of Monroe, Maine and the area was growing. They had a paper mill and shoe factories and all the industries that supported the growing industries. The town of Palmyra had a tannery that supplied leather to the shoe factory. The area was covered with forest and many men worked in the woods, supplying lumber for building, hardwood for furniture and of course pulp wood for the paper mill. It was a glorious time to be in Maine, according to Arthur.

Everything he said in the letter made Alvin feel better about the decision to go and Kellen was ready the moment the plan was presented. He would have hopped a ship with the clothes on his back, but Alvin was deliberate, too much was at stake to make any rash moves.

Kellen never bought any land and had still been saving for a plot on the water, but the prices kept rising along the water and his wait for a bargain grew more and more unlikely with each passing day. America sounded like the place for him. The way Arthur told it, opportunity abounded, and all a man need do is show up for work and he'd be set up as a *'gentleman in earnest'*. Alvin was pretty sure Arthur stole that term from Treasure Island which was his favorite book as a child.

Whether it was true or not, Alvin liked the idea of starting a new life. He loved Ireland, but it was just a place, and many thousands of Irish had moved to America. To his knowledge, none had ever returned. He figured there must have been some, but none that he knew. Certainly no one from the village had ever returned. There must be something to it if everybody stayed. The one thing that puzzled Alvin was Arthur's suggestion that they bring as many clothes as they owned. Weren't there clothes in America? He thought. It seemed odd.

Kellen may have been on board, but when it came to Emma and Jameson, Annie was not. They were still children in her eyes and needed their family.

Alvin sat with Emily and Jameson outside the cottage and listened are the battle over their futures rage on.

Ambrose drummed his fingers on the table. "What will he do if he stays? Cut peat? Farm sheep? Fish? That's all this place has to offer Annie."

Annie stiffened and pointed at Ambrose. "He's not going, and neither is Emily. When they are grown, they can make their own choices, but until then they need to be here. With us. Let the boys go off and see if it's the paradise McCall makes it to be or just some drunken fantasy of his. You know he's fond of the poteen and any other drink he can get his hands on."

"For the love of Christ woman. Paper mills and shoe factories aren't drunken fantasies. They are actual places. He's not saying its Shangri-La, it's a just a town in America."

Annie's face started to redden, and he could see tears starting to form with her frustration. Ambrose realized that this was not some irrational fear driving her opposition. It was the thought of losing her family. She expected grandchildren someday and her first one died with Edna. Now both Alvin and Kellen would be gone and any of their children would be born on the other side of the world. She might go the rest of her life without ever seeing them. She couldn't stop the boys, they were both adults and would do what they wanted, but the others were still children, and she lived to be a mother. When the first teardrop rolled down her cheek, Ambrose knew that he had lost the argument.

He stood and moved next to her pulling her head to his body. "I understand, love... They'll stay."

The trio listening from outside heard the verdict and Jameson's face fell from optimism to defeat. Alvin put his arm around him. "Be a good lad and before you know it, you can come to America too. We'll get a place with enough rooms for everyone."

Jameson nodded, but didn't speak as he fought back the urge to cry.

Emily hugged her brother. "Cheer up Jamie. We can start saving now and go there ourselves one day. Maybe Ma and Da will come too and then we can all live there, just like here."

Jameson frowned. "They'll never leave here. Which means we'll never leave either."

Now Alvin frowned. "You can spend your next few years being angry about not going, or you can plan and prepare for your journey. When you're a man, you can do what you want, and we'll be there. Or you can look at other places, like Boston or New York. But what I will tell you is resentment won't get you there any faster, it will only make teh wait seem longer."

Jameson heard what he was trying to say. It didn't make him feel any better, but he understood.

❀ ❀ ❀ ❀

Richard had been away in England since the end of the summer but liked to come to the manor house for the holidays. Alvin saw Smith buying supplies in the village, so he knew that Richard would be arriving soon.

"Good morning Mr. Smith!" Alvin called from across the lane.

Smith looked around, and a broad smile crossed his face when he saw Alvin. "Well, young McGinn, there you are. His lordship will be wanting to see you when he arrives tomorrow. He said that he received your letter, and he would like you to come to the house for dinner in the evening if you are free."

Alvin looked up and smiled. "Are you heading in that direction now? I was going back to the cottage and would appreciate a ride part of the way."

Smith pulled the hand brake. "Jump up here then, and we'll be on our way."

Alvin climbed onto the bench and Smith released the brake and started the team forward again.

Smith looked forward as he drove. "So, how are things with you?"

Alvin knew what he was asking. How were things without Edna? He paused for a long moment. "I miss her terribly. I took to drink for a while, but that didn't seem to help."

Smith laughed. "It never does. There's nothing wrong with a drink now and then, but I can assure you. No one has ever found the solution to their problem in the bottom of a bottle."

"I'm learning that lesson. I'm looking to sell my place and move to America. We have friends there and they say there's plenty of work for everyone."

Smith contemplated on that for a moment. "I suppose there is. The country is enormous. It's bigger than England, France, Spain and Germany combined."

"Has his Lordship been there before? We've never talked about it."

"Yes. He was in New Brunswick, Canada, and then in Boston about two years ago. He has a business interest in a Canadian railroad of some sort. I know little about it except the plan is to have the railroad stretch all the way across Canada."

Alvin tried to picture a map of Canada and how far the railway would have to stretch. It seemed like an impossible distance. The thought of trains passing through forests and over mountains was mind-boggling to him. No wonder they must need so much labor, he thought. It would take years to complete, even with thousands of men working on it.

"That's incredible. It would be like building a railroad from here to Africa."

"I suppose it would."

Alvin looked around as they rode. "Is her ladyship and her sister coming as well?"

Smith grinned. "Not for several days yet. They'll come closer to the actual holiday. His lordship is always in a much better mood without her hanging on his shoulder like impending doom."

Alvin disliked how they made him feel. He always felt like he was intruding when they were around, and he would never forget how they made Edna feel when they had first met them. They were judgmental and yet somehow seemed insecure at the same time.

He knew he'd miss Richard whenever he actually moved. It seemed like such a trivial thing the day he helped him in the street, but from that moment, he had never had a better friend. Alvin still didn't know why, except that Richard had no friends. All Alvin knew was that for all of his wealth and privilege, he had a big heart. He had been genuinely happy when Alvin and Edna married, then equally devastated when she passed. Alvin felt sorry for him in some ways. As long as he was trapped in his arranged marriage, he would never know the love Alvin had shared with Edna.

Twenty-Six

Alvin sat in the parlor of the manor house waiting for Richard. The house was impressive, even though the surrounding counties boasted larger homes. Alvin was fascinated by the ornate woodwork. The room was framed in dark wainscot panels and the corners of each door were decorated with a rampant lion arranged in a way that they faced each other like in the Ellingwood coat of arms. A fire was burning hot in the fireplace, and the entire room had a faint smell of leather and tobacco smoke.

White stepped in to announce that Richard would be down soon. "Could I interest you in some cognac? His lordship has asked me to pour some for him."

"Yes, please. I could use a small drop of something."

White opened a cabinet and pulled two crystal glasses and a decanter from a shelf. He poured a generous shot into each glass and placed them on a silver try to carry them across the room. He placed Alvin's glass on the table beside him, then stood erect.

"Mr. McGinn. I would like to offer my sincere condolences on the loss of your wife and child. She was one of the kindest people I have ever met and treated me like a gentleman."

Alvin looked at White and could see that he was fighting back tears a bit. "She was kind indeed, and she did like you very much and found your story interesting. Thank you for telling me. It makes my heart fuller to hear of all the people who loved her."

White forced a grin and gave a light bow of his head, then took his station near the door holding the tray. A few seconds later, Alvin could hear Richard coming down the stairs. He stepped across the threshold and took the drink from the tray. "Thank you White. That will be all for now." White left and closed the door behind him.

Richard stepped forward and raised his glass. "Alvin. I'm happy to see you, my friend."

Alvin raised his glass in return. "I'm always happy to see you too, Richard. Thank you for having me."

Richard dragged a leather chair a closer to the fire and nodded toward another one. "Pull that one over and sit with me. I'm still cold from my journey. The damp seems to have crept into my bones."

Alvin dragged the chair closer, and the two men drank toasts to each other's health.

Richard watched the fire through his glass of cognac. "I received your letter. Where do you want to go when you get to America? I've been to Boston. It's a very busy place. I don't think you'd care for it much. It's crowded and very dirty."

"Maine. We have friends from the village that moved there about ten years ago."

"Ah. That's a fine choice. It's mostly wilderness, but it's growing. It borders New Brunswick. I have a business interest there. I am a major shareholder in the Canadian Pacific Railway."

"That's impressive."

"Not really. But it is a sound investment. Railways are typically a strong investment. Have you ever heard of the American, Conelius Vanderbilt?"

Alvin blushed a little. "I'm sorry, I don't know that I have. Is he a railroad man?"

"Yes, and shipping as well. He's probably the biggest in the world. If you move materials or products in America, you'll probably do it on a Vanderbilt train or ship."

Alvin's mind went to a map of America again. "That's incredible."

"It is. That's why we are copying his process to some degree. We not only own the Canadian Pacific Railway, but we have purchased two ships as well to ferry materials and passengers back and forth between Liverpool and Quebec City, although in the winter, we only travel as far as St. John, New Brunswick because of the ice."

"Ice?" Alvin said and sipped his drink.

"Yes. It gets so cold that the ice will swallow a ship up and it will be there until spring unless the pressure crushes the hull and then the entire ship is lost. You should see the great animal pelts some people wear. Black bear skins so large, they cover a man from shoulders to heels. Which reminds me. Bring as many clothes as you can. If you dress in layers, you'll be much warmer."

Alvin could feel it becoming harder to breathe and realized he was anxious. "McCall said that too. What does it look like there if it's that cold? Are there houses like here?"

Richard drained his drink and watched the crystal refract light in the fire. "Yes. Different styles of houses because they have more wood than you can possibly conceive. Forests so vast you could walk for weeks and never get to a clearing. That's why we need the railways, to transport wood from the interior to the coast."

"I can't even imagine it. No wonder no one comes back to Ireland." Alvin finished his drink and placed the glass on the table.

Richard pushed himself up out of the chair and retrieved the decanter from the cabinet. "I don't want to keep calling White, I'm certain we're capable of pouring our own drinks," he said with a laugh. He poured another drink for Alvin and one for himself. "So, I imagine you are going to sell the cottage and the land?"

Alvin looked at the floor. "I would like to, but I would never want to offend you."

Richard laughed. "My friend. That was a gift to do with as you please. You could have sold it the day I gave it to you. I told you that before. Wilkes said that you refused their offer of four pounds per acre."

"I did. I had plans for that place. To make a life with Edna and I did that, but now that she's gone, I don't like to be there at all. I tend the flock, but then I walk to the village or my folks or just walk."

"I think I'd feel the same way if I were you." Richard sipped his drink. "Have you looked for buyers yet?"

"I haven't. The last time I saw Mr. Booth he told me that the prices were dropping because no one was buying, and some farmers were beginning to default on their loans."

Richard laughed and his enormous belly shook the drink he was resting on it. "Nonsense. There are always buyers. He's just hoping you'll sell to him at a bargain. I believe that they are getting three pounds, fifteen shillings per acre. That should make your property worth one hundred and fifty pounds, more or less. We'll talk about a plan for Mr. Booth before you leave."

"Well, I have a loan with them for seven pounds for the new roof as well, but one hundred and forty-three pounds is a small fortune. Do you think it will buy anything in America?"

"It will buy plenty. Especially in a place like Maine. Land is inexpensive there. Every hundred pounds is worth about five-hundred of their American dollars."

Alvin could have been knocked over with the lightest of touch. He had never dreamed that he would go to America with so much. But then he thought about the journey and all the points that he might be swindled or robbed. "I'll be a wreck carrying a large sum like that. It could get lost or stolen."

Richard smiled, but didn't laugh at his friend. His life was spent around finance, so it was amusing to speak with someone who had never held a bank account. "You can take a small sum with you, and we can do a wire transfer for the balance when you reach Maine." He could see by the blank look on Alvin's face that he had never heard of the process. "When you get to Maine, you will go to a telegraph office and send a message. Then the bank here will transfer the money to the bank there. It's much safer than carrying cash or promissory notes that can be lost or stolen."

"What an amazing world we live in that we can send messages across the ocean in an instant. We sent a letter, and it took weeks to get a response. What bank do I use?"

Richard sipped his drink. "Wilkes and Boothe can do it, but if you'd prefer, when the time comes, I'll use my bank in London. I can have the papers drawn up and the money will be there when you arrive."

"Thank you, Richard. You are a great friend."

"Well, you did save my life that day."

"Honestly..."

Richard held up a hand. "I know you didn't actually save my life, but I appreciated that you cared for me like a friend. I have more money than I can spend in ten lifetimes, but what I don't have are people who actually care about me and that day you cared. I sent the land gift so that we might become friends in life."

"I would have been your friend without the gift, I hope you know that."

Richard smiled. "I do. That's why I gave it to you. I'm glad that you shared it with Edna. My heart hurts just thinking about her. The world is worse off without her in it." He looked at his drink. "May we toast her?"

Alvin was startled by the question. "Of course."

"Sweet Edna, may you always keep watch over this man and keep your light shining down upon him."

Alvin felt his eyes start to burn. "To Edna."

They raised their glasses and drank.

Twenty-Seven

The bell rang over the door at Wilkes & Booth as Alvin crossed the threshold. In the corner of the room a fire roared in the stove, making the room intensely warm after coming in from the cold. James Booth stood comparing papers to a ledger book. At the sound of the bell, he looked up and his face changed from one of intense concentration to one of false civility. Alvin recognized it well now. It was the look Booth used to deliver the news that he was about to try to cheat you.

"Well, the indentured servant has returned." Booth's cat-like grin turned to a full smile. "Do you need to borrow more money. For the holiday perhaps?"

"No, I am here to discuss terms for selling the property."

Booth stood up straighter and took on a more serious countenance. "Are you now? Why the change in heart?"

Alvin felt embarrassed that he would have to talk about losing Edna again since he might burst into tears at the very mention of her, but he resolved not to let Booth get the best of him. "Ever since my wife and child passed, I have no joy at that place. That's all I need to say about it."

"Yes. Of course. How indelicate of me. I recall her funeral procession, it was an impressive spectacle for someone so young. Generals in England had less turn out in London than that woman did here. Do you have a buyer?"

"No. I thought to come here first since you had offered before."

Booth feigned looking kindly. "That's right. I think you turned down four pounds an acre if I recall. That was a very generous offer."

"At the time I was building a life here. Now that time has passed."

Booth nodded and opened the ledger to the page with the tables for current values. "Well now, let's see where things stand. We've had a high number of defaulters, so that hasn't helped things." Booth ran his finger down the column and shook his head. "I'm afraid you'll be a bit disappointed. The most I can offer is two pounds, ten shillings an acre. That's a hundred pounds. A very impressive sum for a *gift*, wouldn't you say."

Alvin was expecting this. "I would. I have been talking with people around here and I know what you are doing. You are taking the land back and letting the farmers stay on as tenants. You're making yourself to be the new lord here."

"Well now lad. I recall you said you were a student of history. I am a student of finance. Men sign on for an obligation and when they fail to meet their obligation, they forfeit the object.

But an unworked farm is no use to anyone. So, these people you are talking with, should learn a little about finance before they slander legitimate businesses. Because you have always been a fair man to deal with, the best I'll do is two pounds, fifteen shillings, which would be one hundred and ten pounds leaving you with one hundred and three after clearing your debt with us. Now how can you argue with that?"

"I was instructed not to take less than three pounds, ten shillings an acre and the debt forgiven because the money went into fixing the property and increased the value by having a livable cottage."

Booth laughed out loud and slammed him ledger shut. "Well now Mr. McGinn. I'm not sure which one of the barstool solicitors at the public house advised you of that, but I can assure you that those numbers don't work for me, and I dictate the terms, not you."

Now it was Alvin's turn to smile. "I'm most heartily sorry you feel that way. You see, the solicitor you spoke of was his lordship and he gave me the advice over dinner last evening at the Manor House."

Booth's arrogance melted like a frost on a windowpane when the morning sun delivered its kiss.

"He also said to give you this," Alvin produced a sealed envelope and handed it to Booth, "and if you don't comply fully with his instructions, he'll be down himself to change the name of this office to Wilkes."

Booth studied the rampant lions facing each other on the seal and knew it immediately to be legitimate.

"When all is said and done, it is his lordships money, so he can spend it as he pleases. I can draw papers up and have the money wired to a bank for you. There is a small fee of six percent for wire transfers through our office." Booth looked anxious for a reply since any glimmer of profit was melting away as fast as his arrogance.

Alvin, grinned and held out his hand. "That won't be necessary, his lordship will arrange the transfer from his bank in London once I arrive in Maine."

Booth shook his hand. "Oh, Maine you say. I hear it's lovely there. Hard winters, but four complete seasons. Far less rain than here too. I take it the instructions for sale are in the envelope?"

"They are. Three pounds, ten per acre and forgiveness of my loan."

Booth placed the envelope on the desk. "You're a lucky man to have friends like this."

Alvin smiled and nodded. "Yes, I am."

※ ※ ※ ※

Annie, Emily and Jameson arrived at the cottage a little after breakfast to help Alvin pack up the cottage. He had offered to send Edna's clothes back to the Collins' but Paddy didn't see the need and now Emily was to inherit the clothes. He hadn't been able to buy her any jewelry so there nothing to give away.

When they packed up the kitchen, Alvin looked at the three teacups and saucers and his mind was dragged back to the broken cup on the floor. "I don't want those back. Emily can have them."

"Are you sure? They were a gift. We could always find a replacement and ship them to you once you're settled," asked Annie.

"No Ma. I don't care for the pattern anymore."

"Well, you really don't have a lot here, son. It won't even fill the cart."

"I have nothing of value except for clothes and a few trinkets. Everyone says to bring warm clothes, so maybe those are the most valuable."

The cottage was empty, and Jameson was loading some tools from the shed onto the cart. "Do you want those carved wood pieces for anything? They look like they go to a chair."

"It was a crib...and no you can leave them. The only things I'm leaving here with are memories."

Jameson loaded the last box. "I believe that's it."

Alvin looked around. That was it. His whole life fit in the back of a wagon with room to spare. "Head for home and I'll be along after I meet with Duffy."

The little cart and his family started away, and he watched them until they were out of sight. He went to the shed and removed a board that laid between two studs. A quart bottle of brown ale rested behind it. Alvin wiped the top on his shirt to remove the dust and gripped the cork with his teeth and twisted. The bottle popped and a little foam rose to the top, trickling over. Alvin sipped the foam up and walked outside with the bottle in hand.

Sean was walking up the road with another man and a black and white dog. Kelly sprang to mind, but the man wasn't Carrigan. The person was a stranger to him.

Sean called and waved. "Morning, McGinn!" Alvin waved and closed the distance between them.

"Morning, Sean."

"It's a bit early for the drink, isn't it?" asked Sean.

"After you take these sheep, and this cow. I've no more work today, so why not? It's my last bottle. You want some?"

Duffy smiled. "Yes, of course I do. What is it?"

"Brown Ale."

"That'll work." He took the bottle and had a drink from the bottle and handed it back. "Alvin. This is Peter Murphy. He's going to use his dog to herd the flock to my place."

When he handed it back, Alvin offered it to Murphy. "Peter, care for a drink?"

Murphy held up a hand. "No thanks lad, I'm not much of a drinker."

"Fair enough...what's your dog's name?"

"Lucky... He's lucky I don't sell him to the Gypsies. He only listens about half the time, but he is a good worker, that is when he decides to work."

Murphy said something to the dog in Irish and Lucky took off across the pasture and started gathering the sheep. Watching him herd the flock to the gate was like watching a four-legged ballet. Murphy stood and blocked the road to the right and waved a long staff guiding the sheep to the left back toward Duffy's.

Sean turned to Alvin. "Is there anything left inside?"

"No, it's all on the wagon you passed on the way here."

"I'd hate to seem superstitious, but go back inside, look around and come out again, and be sure that every window and the door is shut. Bad luck can follow a man if you leave one open."

Alvin studied Sean in case he was playing a prank, but he could see by his expression that he was serious. Alvin wasn't superstitious by nature, but he had experienced enough bad luck for a lifetime this year.

He went into the house and walked around once. "Edna, if you're in here love, leave now. I'd hate to have you trapped here." Alvin stepped outside and closed the door behind him.

Sean smiled. "There. You should be safe now. Now come along and you'll say goodbye to Mrs. Duffy on the way by."

They walked toward Duffy's farm and Sean handed Alvin a small satchel of coins as payment for the sheep. "That should get keep you fed on your way to America."

Alvin put the coins in his pocket. Sean had been a true friend to him, and he'd never discredit him by counting the sum. If it was short, he didn't care.

Sean held a hand and pointed. "Look at that," he whispered.

"What am I looking at?" Alvin whispered back.

"Magpies in that tree right there. That's a good sign for you."

Alvin had heard that magpies were lucky omens and that you could lift a curse by waving at them, but he knew little more than that.

"Do you know the rhyme?" asked Sean still whispering.

"No. I can't say that I do."

"One for sorrow, two for joy. Three for a girl, and four for a boy. Five for silver, six for gold. Seven for a secret never to be told."

"I've never heard that before."

"Get ready to wave." Sean clapped his hand loudly and hooted. The birds beat out from the tree and flew away from them. "Wave now!"

Alvin waved. He felt foolish waving to birds, but who was he to tempt fate? "It looked like over seven. What does that mean?"

"I think it means that you'll be just fine in America. You'll have a good life there."

Alvin smiled. "I hope you're right Sean."

Twenty-Eight

The day was unusually warm for January and the sun felt good on Alvin's face. He and Kellen were leaving for Liverpool today and the family loaded the donkey cart with a trunk that stored the boy's belongings. Nothing of great value, but it was most everything they owned.

Richard had arranged the for the bulk of Alvin's money to be wired when they reached America and as a favor, he did the same for Kellen. The sum was far smaller, but the ability to keep the money safe meant a lot to Kellen. Alvin left twenty pounds with his parents to help pay for Emily and Jameson's passage to America if they ever decided to leave Ireland, and Ambrose agreed to leave it in a bank until the time came that they could leave.

The Harp sisters had come for Christmas and Richard left with them just prior to New Year's Eve so that they could celebrate the New Year in London. He sent a goose to Alvin's parents' house for the family to have for Christmas dinner. Richard was a good man, and Alvin was going to miss him. They had agreed that when Richard had business in New Brunswick or Boston, he would try to notify Alvin well in advance so that they might connect. Richard even wanted to see his place in Maine some day when he was finally settled.

They walked along making small talk and laughing about sea sickness and people wearing animal skins in Canada. Alvin saw a flash from the corner of his eye and a robin landed on a post at the side of the road. He thought about what Edna had said about her grandmother. Maybe it's Edna, he thought. The bird looked at the party and flew off down the road.

The road was soft from a rain that had fallen during the night and mud started to cake on the wheels. "Jameson, when we get to the village find a stick to scrape these wheels a bit or we'll be pushing the cart along with the donkey," said Ambrose.

"I will, Da," replied Jameson.

Alvin felt a little sorry for him. Jameson wanted to go to America, but Annie wouldn't have it. Now he was going to be stuck doing the bulk of the physical work along with Ambrose. He was already working in the peat bog a couple of days a week. *I imagine he's counting down the days already*, he thought.

"Jameson, what do you want from America? I'll send you something when we get there."

"Do they still have Indians there, like in The Last of the Mohicans? I read that book, and I want a tomahawk, like Hawkeye."

Alvin thought for a moment and realized that he didn't know if they still had Indians in Maine. Richard had said it was a wilderness. Maybe they still did. "I don't know if they still have Indians, but if they do, I'll see if they will sell me a tomahawk."

"I want something a lady would like," added Emily.

"I'll see if I can find you something special that you can wear."

When they came into the village, the robin was there again, sitting on a branch near a bench that he and Edna had sat on when he first started courting her and he was convinced it was her.

The cart rumbled by, and the bird flew off toward the docks. He tried to follow its flight, but it rounded a corner and was out of sight.

Kellen had been unusually quiet this morning. Alvin had expected him to be excited about the trip, but perhaps the fear of the unknown was weighing on his mind. They had booked Steerage passages from Liverpool to Canada on the Empress of Ireland which was owned by the Canadian Pacific Railroad. They used it to ferry labor from the United Kingdom to Canada to work on building their railways. The second-class tickets were sold out when they booked their passage and that was just as well. The fare was five pounds each for steerage and more than twice that for second-class. The first-class tickets were far out of reach, so Alvin never even asked.

Steerage would be just like it sounded. They would be crammed into the bowels of the boat like animals along with hundreds of other men, women and children. The fare offered

THE ROBIN'S GAZE

no meals or bedding, so Alvin and Kellen each packed a blanket and some food. The passage was advertised as four nights to make the crossing, but everyone advised them to bring some extra food to barter or in case weather caused a delay.

They arrived at the dock and people were just beginning to board the ferry to Liverpool and they had plenty of time to spare. Alvin and Kellen unloaded the trunk and placed their bags on top of it. They had decided on one bag each to limit their need to carry more than was necessary.

Alvin closed his eyes and looked up to feel the sun on his face. When he looked down and opened his eyes, the robin was sitting on a barrel. *Come to say goodbye?* He wondered. He watched the bird and smiled. He was startled when he heard a loud voice call out, "McGinns!"

It was Paddy, Ellen and the boys. "We have a little something for you lads," Paddy said, and Finn produced a basket with a lid. "It's salted fish. Some cheese, honey and black currant jam. Edna said it was your favorite."

Alvin looked over to the barrel and the robin was still there. He turned back to the Collins'. "Thank you all."

"Well, you can't leave hungry. It may be a while before you can get a proper Irish meal again, so hopefully that will hold you over."

Alvin placed the basket on the trunk and turned to the robin. "Do you see that robin?"

Paddy looked over and then turned to Alvin. "Of course I do. It's ten feet away."

"Once when Edna and I were walking, a robin followed us, and she said it was her gram. Ellen's mother."

Paddy frowned a little, "that's just a superstition son."

Alvin turned to the bird again and smiled. "I know... But what if it's true? This bird has followed us all morning."

"I don't believe in that sort of thing. But I hope I'm wrong. It'd be good to see her from time to time."

Both men watched the bird and to Alvin, the robin's gaze seemed something more lifelike. It watched them back for a few moments and then flew off further down the dock. Neither man spoke, they just watched it go.

Paddy pulled his pipe and a leather bag of tobacco from his coat pocket. "Have a smoke with me before you go?"

"I will." Alvin pulled his pipe and loaded it from a bag in his pocket. Paddy lit Alvin's pipe and then his own.

"You're a good lad. I'm proud to say that you were my son-in-law. I can see why she loved you."

Alvin felt tears starting to burn his eyes. This was probably the last time he'd see any of the Collins'. "I was proud to call you father."

Looking at Alvin made the rock like Paddy start to well up. When he realized what was happening, he stiffened. "This damned breeze is blowing the smoke right in my eyes."

Alvin chuckled and sniffled. "Mine too and it's making my nose run."

Paddy extended a hand and Alvin looked him in the eyes and shook it. He had thought to speak, but he didn't need to. This was goodbye. When he let go of Alvin's hand, Paddy turned and called out, "Come along boys, these fish aren't catching themselves."

Sean, Finn and Ellen all said their goodbyes and followed Paddy back down the lane.

Kellen looked around and saw that the gangway was clear. "It's time."

They kissed their mother and hugged Emily and Jameson. Ambrose shook their hands one last time and each man grabbed a handle on the trunk, then they made their way up the gangway.

Alvin produced the tickets for passage, and they stood at the siderail. Watching the people they loved.

"Do you think we'll ever see Ma or Da again?" asked Kellen.

"I don't know. I doubt I'll ever come back. I hope that someday they'll all come over. But Ma is stubborn, and Da will do as he's told."

Kellen chuckled. "Take a good look then."

"I will."

Alvin studied his family and forced a smile as he waved. He was eager for his new adventure, but part of him would miss the Ireland he had known. From their vantage point he could see most of the village. He looked at the tree near the church, but he couldn't see Francis. He saw a man with a dog and hoped it was Kelly, but it was another farmer and another dog.

Behind his family he could see the barrels and the robin was sitting there again. This time it was joined by a second one. *Her Gram, or maybe Nora*, he thought and smiled.

A horn blew and the ferry started moving. At the sound the two robins jumped into the air and flew toward the lane where the Collins' live. "Watch over them," he said aloud.

"Watch over who?" asked Kellen.

"All of them."

Author's Message

When I started the McGinn Family Saga series, I never expected to go beyond those books. But when people asked what's next? I really didn't have an answer. The answer came when I started working on a pilot for a TV series based upon The Red Road. Where the book starts on the night Jim is walking home in the rain, we actually started the pilot in the morning of that day.

This made me think about events that would have led up to the start of those books. I went back to Alvin and how he might have come from Ireland and then all of the historical events that happened between 1910 and 1933. World War I, prohibition, pandemics and of course the great depression. This book begins Alvin's journey and will carry on for at least two more books and possibly other books in the world of the fictional Monroe, Maine.

Whoa, wait. Did he say TV series? I did. In the Summer of 2023, I was approached by a screenwriter about making the book into a pilot and from there we joined forced with a Hollywood producer. The script was written in 2023, and we created a podcast in the summer of 2024 to help sell the concept to film production companies. A link to the podcast is available on my website. The process has been both fascinating and fun, but it did cause a significant delay in the release of this book and the next two volumes in this series.

Thank you sincerely for waiting, and for your continued support and I will do my best to keep the stories coming.

Jon

About the Author

Jonathan McCarthy is a Maine native who has a deep appreciation for the state's rich characters and natural beauty. Growing up in Maine, he developed a strong connection to the land and its people, and these experiences have influenced his writing.

Jon's work often explores the complexities of human relationships and the ways in which people and families are shaped by their surroundings. He is particularly interested in the unique culture and history of Maine, and many of their stories are set in small towns and rural communities throughout the state.

Through his writing, the author strives to capture the spirit of Maine and the people who call it home. He believes that storytelling is a powerful way to connect with others and to create a sense of community, and they hope that their work will inspire readers to explore the beauty and complexity of this remarkable state.

If you enjoyed this book, please take the time to leave a review where you purchased it.

Please check out my website

http://jemccarthy-author.com

for information and special offers on future books and other media!

Thank you and happy reading!

Jon

Also by

The McGinn Family Saga Series

The Red Road

First Place Winner, Fall 2023 Historical Fiction BookFest
First Place Winner, Debut Novel 2023 Literary Global Book Awards
First Place Winner, Best Fiction-Northeast 2024 Indie Author Book Awards

There's no greater duty than family...

In the heart of rural Maine, in the midst of the Great Depression and the final year of Prohibition, the McGinn family stands at a crossroads. The bond between Alder, Finn, and Lewin McGinn, the oldest sons of a widowed mother raising twelve children, is about to be tested in ways they could never have imagined.

Their central desire is to seek justice for their brother Jim's mysterious killing, but the primary challenge lies in the fact that the local authorities lack the evidence to bring anyone to justice. With their small, close-knit community paralyzed by fear, the McGinn brothers take it upon themselves to unravel the truth, even if it means taking the law into their own hands.

As the Morelands, the wealthiest family in town, reveal themselves as the primary villains in this historical family saga, a twist emerges that elevates the stakes even higher. The Morelands are not just influential landowners; they are also the major bootleggers in the area, orchestrating a sprawling empire under the shadow of Prohibition. June 1933 sets the stage for a climactic showdown in Central Maine, where the McGinns and the Morelands vie for power, justice, and survival.

"The Red Road" is not just a tale of survival and trust but a profound exploration of family bonds and the sacrifices one makes when duty calls. As the McGinn brothers devise a plan to bring down the Moreland empire, they face a moral dilemma - what lengths are they willing to go to for the sake of justice? Dive into the intricate world of "The Red Road" and join the McGinn family as they fight for what's right, uncovering the secrets that lie hidden beneath the surface. In a time when no duty is greater than family, the McGinns will inspire you with their unwavering determination to seek the truth.

The Mothers McGinn

First Place Winner, Fall 2023 Book Fest Award: Family Saga

Every wedding seems like the beginning of a fairy tale, but sometimes the prince is actually a frog, or the big bad wolf.
When Mary McGinn lost her husband, she was the mother of twelve children, and her oldest sons worked to provide for the family. She was always grateful for the sacrifices her children had made for the sake of their family, but now she needed to go back to work so that they could go on and live their lives. But finding work in depression-stricken Maine would not be easy for anyone in 1935, perhaps even more so for a woman.
Mary's oldest daughter Allison and son Lewin both get married and find out that marriage is fraught with challenges, sometimes from inside the home and sometimes from outside. Dealing with alcoholism, trauma, and motherhood is all it takes to bring the fairy tales back to reality.
Follow the McGinn family through trials and triumphs as the children become adults and couples become families in the Mothers McGinn.

Counting Crossroads

Winner First Place BookFest Spring 2024: Multi-period Family Saga

When alone in our thoughts, the mind turns to memories and choices made at the many crossroads in life.

The world is changing fast for the McGinns; they have electricity and with that comes a radio to hear the news of the world. But the news outside of Maine is not very happy. The third book in the McGinn family saga follows the lives of the siblings' growth to adulthood, and the many challenges that come with the adult world. Mary relies on tradition and strength to shepherd her flock through marriages and death in Depression era, Maine. Jobs are still scarce, but the McGinn family keeps growing and the family members work to find their place in the world. Mary McGinn finds herself faced with an alcoholic son-in-law and a grandchild suffering from a childhood illness. Patrick becomes restless with life on the farm, which threatens to drive a wedge between him and his closest brother Alston.

Finn and Ruth meet the loves of their lives and the Moreland Store turns into Moreland corner, complete with new businesses to serve the people who live out of town. Their happiness is short-lived however, when Albert Merrill is released from prison and once again puts himself on a collision course with the Morelands and McGinns.

Come along on this journey and follow the McGinns from the late 1930s to the absolute brink of World War Two.

The Warrior's Wounds

BookFest Fall 2024 Winner of two First Place Medals (Historical Fiction War & Military) and one Second Place Medal (Multi-period Family Saga)

Sometimes the wounds you can't see leave the deepest scars.

In the throes of World War II, Mary McGinn finds herself at the heart of a global conflict, not on the front lines, but in the quiet battlefields of her own home. Widowed and left to raise twelve children on her own, Mary's life becomes a tapestry woven with threads of love, sacrifice, and unwavering determination.

As the McGinn men scatter across the globe to serve in various branches of the military, Mary and the other McGinn women grapple with the fear of the unknown, the anguish of separation, and the constant specter of loss. From the battlefields of Europe to the Pacific islands, her sons face the brutal realities of war, each carrying with them a piece of home that makes them a family.

Yet, amidst the chaos, Mary's spirit remains unbroken. She is the rock. With resilience forged in the fires of adversity, she navigates the challenges of rationing, the torment of not knowing and the ever-present dread of a telegram bearing tragic news.

Through letters exchanged across continents and the silent prayers whispered in the darkness, The McGinn women hold on to hope with a tenacity that defies the chaos of war.

J.E. MCCARTHY

The Warrior's Wounds is a poignant tale of a family's love transcending borders and boundaries, weaving a narrative that celebrates the strength of the human spirit in the face of adversity. It is a testament to the courage, resilience, and enduring bonds that unite families, even in the darkest of times.

Book Two of Alvin's Journey is expected in Spring 2025
Alvin and Kellen set off for America via New Brunswick, Canada. They will cross the Atlantic and the great north woods to seek a new life in the United States.

Made in the USA
Middletown, DE
16 February 2025

Made in the USA
Middletown, DE
24 June 2024

FREE BONUS CHAPTER

Unlock the secrets to avoiding costly IT blunders with an exclusive bonus chapter, **"The Top 10 Mistakes Business Owners Make With IT."**

Don't let your business fall victim to security breaches, inefficient processes, or outdated technologies. This bonus chapter reveals the most common pitfalls companies face when managing IT, and how to avoid them.

From implementing scalable solutions to leveraging innovative tech for a competitive edge, this free download is a must-have for anyone serious about mastering information technology management.

Don't miss these pivotal lessons which are available exclusively to our readers. Visit our website now to download your free copy and turn IT challenges into opportunities!

Sign up here: https://NextCenturyTech.com/chapter

Or scan here:

HOW TO MANAGE IT IN YOUR BUSINESS

Zero-day vulnerability: A type of vulnerability that is unknown to the software developer. There is no patch or defense against a hacker who wishes to exploit it. See also security vulnerabilities.

Virtual Private Network: Often referred to as VPN. A VPN is a secure virtual tunnel between two or more computer systems or multiple networks or a combination of multiple computers and networks. The communications are secured with encryption keys to ensure that no one can intercept the communications. See also encryption.

Virtualization: Server virtualization is where a single host computer runs multiple virtual machines (VMs). See Chapter 3 for a detailed analogy of how it works.

Virtual Machine: A computer whose operating system is now virtualized. See virtualization.

Virus: A form of malware that replicates itself. It finds a host operating system (think Windows or Mac) and inserts its own code into operating system files. It can also insert itself into a host program like Word or Excel. They can also be found in spreadsheet macros.

VM or virtual machines: See virtualization.

VPN: See virtual private network.

Vulnerabilities: See security vulnerabilities.

Worm: Standalone malware program designed that can replicate itself. It can use the host system to scan for other vulnerabilities on the network. See also malware and security vulnerabilities.

HOW TO MANAGE IT IN YOUR BUSINESS

Social engineering: Utilizes social and psychological manipulations to trick someone into giving a hacker access to passwords or IT resources they wouldn't normally have access to. Phishing emails fall under social engineering because the email tricks the user into clicking a link and giving up a password or installing malicious software. Other popular methods include impersonating a user over the phone to a help desk to get a password changed or multifactor authentication by-passed.

SSO: See single sign-on

Two-factor authentication: A method by which computers confirm your identity based on exactly two different factors. Those factors could be a username and password plus a 6-digit code texted to your mobile phone. Or it could be as simple as a password plus answering some security questions at login. See also multifactor authentication.

Uninterruptable power supply: A device with a battery that provides power to workstations, servers, switches, firewalls, and any other network hardware. The batteries kick in during power failures. Smart UPS's will properly shut down equipment prior to the battery being drained.

UPS: See uninterruptable power supply.

Security vulnerabilities: Weaknesses in the design of an application or software that allows hackers to gain access to computer systems. There are 4 types: network vulnerabilities, operating system vulnerabilities, process/procedure vulnerabilities, and human vulnerabilities.

Service Organization Control 2: A certification earned by a cloud provider that states their computer systems meets the standard for security, availability, processing integrity, confidentiality or privacy as set by the American Institute of Certified Public Accountants. Why? It means the provider is committed to security. These rigorous standards are added protection for your data.

Single sign-on: The ability to use one set of credentials to log into multiple related or unrelated systems. An example would be using your Facebook credentials to log into Instagram. Many websites offer the ability to sign up with your LinkedIn account or Google or Microsoft365. Also, there are vendors dedicated to providing the single sign-on experience between any two systems including both local and in the cloud. See also OAuth2.0.

SOC2: See Service Organization Control 2.

HOW TO MANAGE IT IN YOUR BUSINESS

Personally identifiable information: Data used to identify a person. That includes full name, address, social security number, driver's license number, financial information, passport, plus many others.

Phishing email: A fake email that appears to be from a legitimate trusted source. There can be several goals of the phish including obtaining a users' login credentials, or personally identifiable information, or bank/credit card number or to click a link that may lead to malware installation. See also personally identifiable information.

PII: See personally identifiable information.

Ransomware: Malicious software designed to encrypt files with the intention of holding them hostage for payment. See also encryption.

Rubber Ducky Attack: Where a USB drive masquerades as a keyboard, which allows it to send commands that appear as keystrokes to the system. Since it simulates a keyboard, USB thumb drive blockers won't stop it.

Security operations center: A manned facility whose job is to live monitor customer's entire IT infrastructure in order to detect hacker attacks and data breaches. Ideally, they have the power to address any such events quickly before damage is done.

authentication is two-factor authentication. See also two-factor authentication.

OAuth2.0: A protocol or framework that provides the ability for one cloud service to authenticate you to a different cloud service. An example would be Facebook asking for access to pictures stored on your iPhone. See also the definition for single sign-on because OAuth is a type of single sign-on.

OCR: See Office for Civil Rights.

Office for Civil Rights: Ran by the US Department of Health and Human Services, the OCR in broad terms protects the civil rights, religious freedoms, and health information privacy of US citizens. In terms of HIPAA, the OCR ensures equal access to health and human services and protects the privacy and security of health information.

Patch panel: Within a data closet, computer room or datacenter, a patch panel bookends those data cable runs that go to the wall jacks in an office or to the wireless access points in the ceiling or any other network-connected device that needs a data cable.

Penetration test: A simulated cyber attack against your computer system to check for exploitable vulnerabilities.

Pentest: See penetration test.

Malware: Any software or application designed to inflict damage or unwanted access or actions on a computer or server. Short for malicious software. Viruses, worms, adware, spyware, and ransomware are all forms of malware.

Managed detection and response: An additional service provided by EDR vendors that provides real-time monitoring and response by a security team in response to incidents identified by the EDR software.

MDR: See managed detection and response.

MFA: See multi-factor authentication.

Microsoft 365 sign-on token: A token is a file that is built after a user successfully authenticates to Microsoft 365 with multifactor authentication. Hackers target these tokens because with it they can bypass multifactor authentication and gain access to 365 mailboxes, SharePoint files and OneDrive files.

Multi-factor authentication: A method by which computers confirm your identity based on at least two different factors, sometimes more. Those factors could be a username and password plus a 6-digit code texted to your mobile phone. Or it could be as complex as a username/password plus a pin plus entering a code from an authentication app on a mobile phone. All *two-factor authentication* is multifactor authentication, but not all multifactor

uses *artificial intelligence* to apply behavioral analytics based on global threat intelligence.

Firewall: A device or software that sits between a computer or network and the internet. The goal of the firewall is to stop hackers from infiltrating the system or network while allowing legitimate data to pass through.

HHS: see Health and Human Services.

Health and Human Services: The US Department of Health and Human Services focuses on the health and well-being of all Americans and provides services related to public health and social services.

Health Insurance Portability and Accountability Act: A federal law that sets guidelines for the protection of patient health information.

HIPAA: see Health Insurance Portability and Accountability Act.

Honeypot: A computer system that appears to be legitimate but is actually a decoy designed to draw the attention of hackers. The software on the honeypot act as a warning system if the hackers infiltrate the network.

Legacy authentication: A method of logging in based on old, outdated and usually poorly secured protocols.

holders are anonymous, which is not entirely true. Holders have pseudonyms, which are traceable to a degree. Many bad actors have been traced via their cryptocurrency transactions.

Cyber extortion: The threat of revealing stolen sensitive data to the public or launching a cyberattack if not paid. A form of blackmail.

Dark web: Websites and content on the internet that is not indexed by conventional search engines like Google, Yahoo, Bing, etc. These sites and content can only be accessed by a specialized browser called The Onion Router or TOR. Its focus is anonymous communications. Often associated with illegal sales and activities, the TOR network is also known for the protection it gives to people under oppressive regimes such as North Korea, China, and Russia.

EDR: See endpoint detection and response.

Encryption: The scrambling of data in a way that can only be undone with the correct key to unscramble it. The key itself is a very long and unique string of letters, numbers, or other characters.

Endpoint Detection and Response: A next-generation antivirus feature that detects threats across the environment and provides in-depth information on how it happened, what files were affected plus an automated response and isolation. It typically

with spam or malicious links in an attempt to take over someone's account or spread false information. Bots can be programmed to attack a website en masse, forcing the site to go offline. This is considered a type of denial-of-service attack.

Browser-in-the-Middle: A fake web server designed to mimic the Microsoft 365 login page. When the victim enters their credentials on the fake page, the sign-in token is stolen.

Brute Force Attack: An automated program or script employed by hackers that tries millions of combinations of letters, numbers, symbols as passwords to gain entry into a computer system.

Cloud: For the purposes of this book, the cloud is a computer or group of computers outside of the organization that provides services to customers. Cloud resources are accessed over the internet, typically via a browser but could also be over a virtual private network or VPN.

Cryptocurrency: A form of currency not tied to a physical object like paper or coins; it's a digital payment system that resides on a network of computers. Cryptocurrency is held in digital wallets. Cryptocurrencies are not tied to physical borders. The first and most popular cryptocurrency is Bitcoin, founded in 2009. Cryptocurrencies helped fuel the age of ransomware. It's often assumed that cryptocurrency

GLOSSARY

2FA: See two-factor authentication.

AI: See artificial intelligence.

Artificial intelligence or AI: A computer or group of computers that make decisions and interactions that are human-like. They can also go a step further and use what they have learned to problem solve and perform tasks that humans would perform. Intelligence attributed to machines rather than a living being.

Bot: Short for robot. A software application that follows a script of tasks. Bots are automated and designed to run without human interaction. Bots are often used for chatting with a website visitor or searching the internet for the best prices. An example of a malicious bot is one that hits social media sites

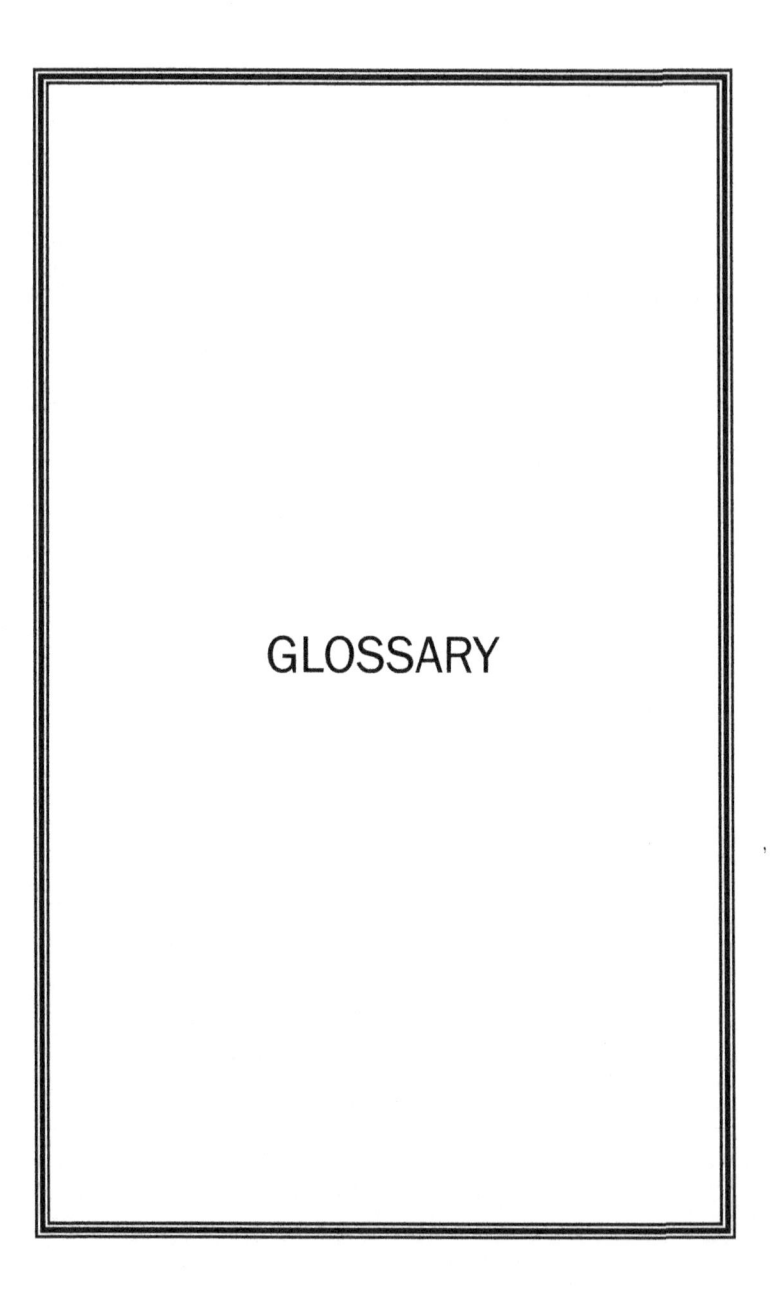

GLOSSARY

PART 4

A SMALL REQUEST

Thank you for reading my book! I am confident you will quickly be able to improve your company's cybersecurity defenses and even share some of the ideas with your fellow business owners and friends.

If possible, could you please leave an honest review of my book on Amazon? Reviews are helpful for others, and I do read them for feedback. Visit:

https://NextCenturyTech.com/ReviewTwo

Networking, problem solving, VoIP, project management, and video editing are her specialties.

Tracy is a 1990 University of Kentucky graduate in Computer Science with Business Specialization. Her various certifications over the years include Novell NetWare, Cisco, A+ and VMware. In 2017, she obtained her drone pilot license.

Tracy and her husband, Joel, have two daughters and a son. She enjoys reading, biking, skiing, scuba, hiking, working with animals, and anything tech.

Find Me:

Website:
https://NextCenturyTech.com

Facebook:
https://facebook.com/NextCenturyTech

LinkedIn:
https://www.linkedin.com/in/NextCenturyTech

ABOUT TRACY HARDIN

Tracy started Next Century Technologies in 2001 (formerly Woodford Computer Solutions) after she was fired from her previous employer, which happened to also be a consulting firm.

She loved the work so much that she went out on her own working from her home office and pickup truck. After the noncompete with her previous employer ended, Tracy was able to resume work for the clients she was serving at her previous employer. Eventually, she could not keep up with the demand, and now Next Century Technologies has a full-time staff and office in Lexington. Nowadays, Tracy's responsibilities include providing guidance for the company, evaluating new technologies, keeping up with cyber threats, implementing new services, marketing, service contracts, and client satisfaction.

3. Do you have a vision of what you would like your IT operations to be?

If you answer yes to all three questions, then let's set up a time to see if we are the right fit for your company. There is no obligation, and scheduling is super easy. During this call, we will explore what your current IT looks like, who is managing it now, what's working and what's not working, and finally, what your goals are. You will also have opportunities to ask questions of me as well. I want to make sure we are both satisfied that we can work together. This is typically a 30- to 45-minute call, but it can be longer if needed to get all your questions and concerns addressed. That's it. No obligation on your part. Here are some ways to reach out to me:

1. Email me at: Tracy@NextCenturyTech.com.

2. Call me at 859-245-0582 and be sure to let my staff know you read my book and want to discuss your IT challenges with me.

3. Schedule a time on my calendar: Visit NextCenturyTech.com and click on the bright yellow box in the bottom right corner titled "Schedule Time Now."

I look forward to hearing from you and possibly working together to make your IT better!

Thank you!

—Tracy Hardin

CHAPTER #9

THE NEXT STEP

I hope this book gave you the knowledge to make better educated decisions for your company's IT. I hope you have already made some of the recommended changes to start improving your operations today.

Still overwhelmed by IT? Need extra help? If the thought of not doing something right worries you, then please reach out to me to see if my team can help.

Before reaching out, please ask yourself these three questions:

1. Do you value your IT and see it as an asset to your company?

2. Are you ready to budget more for your IT expenditures?

HOW TO MANAGE IT IN YOUR BUSINESS

3. **Launch Day**
   - Meet each employee and provide our contact information.
   - Install our monitoring and antivirus agents on each covered computer.
   - Train employees on our ticket portal.
   - Encourage employees to create tickets for issues that need to be addressed.
   - Perform a Security Checklist to see what is missing and what needs to be addressed in a ticket.
   - Finalize backups, if applicable.
   - Install or schedule installation of new hardware, if applicable.

4. **After the Launch.** Our team meets and discusses how the onboarding went and how we can improve it. We then review the Security Checklist and Information Request List plus any other issues with you. Lastly, we update our documentation system.

This is just an overview of a very detailed process we follow to onboard new clients. This process allows us to understand and support our clients' IT infrastructure. Also, by encouraging clients to make tickets, we can start making significant improvements to the computer networks almost immediately.

So, what happens after the ProCare Managed Services Support Agreement is signed?

1. **The Onboarding Meeting.** During our Onboarding meeting, we will:

    - Establish a date of responsibility and a date of launch.

    - Demonstrate our ticket portal.

    - Get old IT provider documentation (if available).

    - Take or ask for pictures of the IT room.

    - For each vendor, find out if we need to be authorized to call in on their behalf. Examples would be the ISP, telcos, and critical line-of-business apps, if applicable.

    - Get an agreement on Security Standards.

    - Find out who approves password changes.

2. **Next Steps.** We then document all the information we have gathered thus far into our documentation system. We set up your company and contacts in our remote monitoring and management software.

Our Elite Plan is great for companies under compliance requirements or who are more risk adverse. It has everything in Standard plus:

- Risk assessment and vulnerability scan.
- Next generation antivirus with EDR and MDR.
- Employee cyber awareness training.
- Dark web monitoring.
- Enterprise password manager for all staff.
- Microsoft 365 advanced threat protection, backups, and monitoring.

Our Bank Compliance Plan is just for banks and credit unions and includes everything in Elite plus:

- Business continuity planning and testing.
- IT audit prep.
- Review of SOC2 vendor reports.
- Level 1 pentest.

All of our plans include a 100% satisfaction guarantee: Give us three months, and if we are not a good fit for your company, then you can cancel.

Next Century's ProCare Managed Services provides proactive management and maintenance of your IT. We get paid to keep everything running smoothly, not just when things go wrong. So, our goal aligns with your goal—maximize computer uptime and network efficiency.

Clients love the fact that their staff can reach out to us directly if a printer stops printing. They get a fast response if the server is down or they forgot a password. If the internet is down, they don't have to call the internet provider and sit on hold; they call us instead. We even help clients save money on their phone and internet bills.

Our ProCare Managed Service plans offer three levels of service because one size does not fit all. Here's a quick summary of each:

Our Standard Plan includes:

- Service Level Agreement—we put what we promise in writing.
- 24/7/365 support.
- Next generation antivirus with EDR.
- Help with picking out hardware, software, and internet.
- Maintenance.
- Management of network devices and servers.
- Microsoft 365 licenses.
- No travel charges if you are local.

CHAPTER #8

PROCARE MANAGED SERVICES BY NEXT CENTURY TECHNOLOGIES

Finding a trusted IT Pro is challenging. If you are hiring your own IT resource, you will discover that demand for IT resources is at an all-time high.

Even if you do pay a high salary, how do you know if this person is really qualified? Do you know what technical questions to ask in an interview? On the other hand, finding a trustworthy IT provider has its own set of challenges. There are so many choices. How do you know which is the best fit for your company and your budget? Do they understand the needs of your particular industry? Are they experienced?

Companies trust us to manage their IT, so they don't have to deal with the hassle of hiring someone or finding a person who has experience. We've been in business since 2001, so you can trust that my team has a lot of experience and a solid client base.

those challenges and are ready to help our clients meet them.

Companies With File Servers

Having file servers in-house creates a challenge when finding good help to manage and protect them. File servers are one of my specialties, so we have extensive experience in managing both stand-alone servers and virtual machines. A server failure can bring a company's day-to-day operations to a halt, so we are the team they can count on to keep the servers going or to recover them quickly if disaster strikes.

Companies With IT Staff

We co-manage IT with companies that an IT person really likes and wants to keep. These business owners understand that their person would benefit from working with my team. We have the tools, processes, and procedures' experience that they may be lacking, and we are happy to share them. We ask their IT person to join our chat channel so they can ask questions easily and get to know my team. Our services allow those IT people to enjoy their time off since we take over the help desk issues while they are gone.

banks. We include time working with the auditors and preparing the reports. We prepare and maintain risk assessments. We provide cyber awareness training for the users. We also perform a level 1 pentest. All the tools we use are picked because they meet the standards required and provide the reports auditors want. Clients rely on us because we have the experience and understand the regulations.

Professional Services

These types of businesses include CPAs, architecture/engineering, veterinarian clinics, construction companies, and financial advisors. These business owners rely heavily on their computers, so their staff needs quick and reliable IT help. We strive to answer 100% of our calls with a live human, and our 24/7 help desk means that those working after hours can still get help. Also, many of these types of companies fall under the Federal Trade Commission (FTC) Safeguards Rule. We understand the guidelines and help companies implement the safeguards they must have in place.

Medical or HIPAA-Covered Entities

Businesses that fall under HIPAA regulations face a lot of regulatory requirements. My company supports several HIPAA-covered entities, so by law, we ourselves fall under HIPAA compliance. We understand

CHAPTER #7

WHO RELIES ON US?

My team and I bring peace of mind to our clients. They know their IT is being managed properly because we meet with them regularly to discuss it.

I would be honored to talk to you about your IT needs whether you already have your own IT Pro or not. To give you a better understanding of what sort of clients we serve, here's a brief overview of some of those that rely on my team for managing IT.

Credit Unions and Community Banks

Credit unions and community banks must follow very specific compliance regulations. We have many years of experience working with these types of institutions. Together with one of our bank clients, we developed a special managed service plan just for

THE PATH FORWARD

PART 3

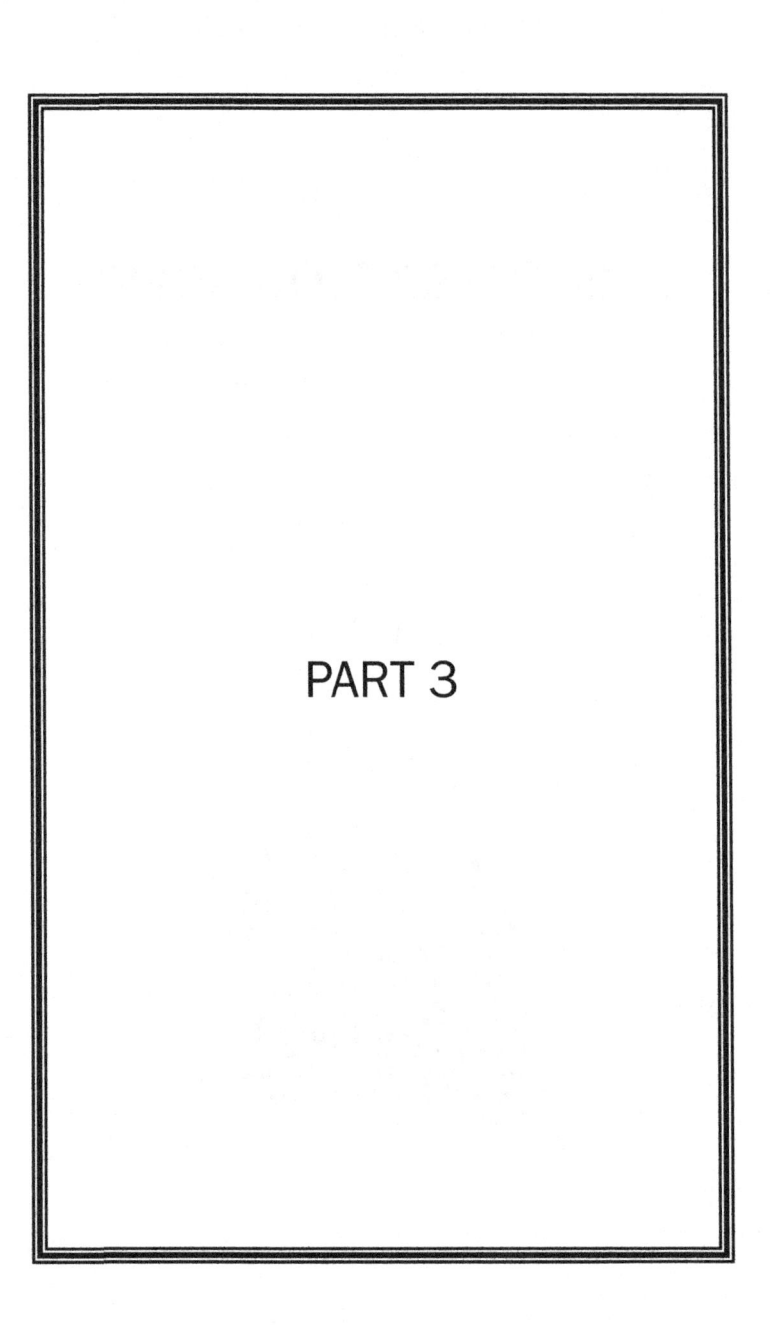

FREE OFFER TO READERS

Sign up for our tech tips!

Each tip takes less than 30 seconds to read but gives you critical info on avoiding online scams, ransom attacks, or other mistakes that can cost you.

Sign up here:

https://NextCenturyTech.com/techtips

Or scan here:

questions and offer recommendations for improving IT. It's wonderful for the in-house staff to just get a second opinion on an idea.

When a potential CoMITs client shows interest, our next step is an in-person or online meeting to determine the best way we can provide support and over what time frame. There will be lots of questions from both parties, and we request basic documentation of your IT assets. An on-site visit is also a must before an agreement is drafted.

- **We are always available.** Since we are a team, you don't have to worry about unavailability due to sick days or vacation.

- **No hiring hassles.** We handle the hiring process and background checks for our new staff, and we have our own training program to get them up to speed.

- **Human resources.** Our great company culture, compensation plan, and benefits keep our staff turnover low. We believe happy employees are critical to good customer service that your staff will appreciate.

- **Less stress.** We help your IT folks implement next-gen cybersecurity protections that prevent or mitigate damages from ransomware or security breach.

- **100% satisfaction guarantee!** We want this to be a win-win situation. If you aren't happy, we aren't happy. All we ask is to give us at least 90 days to make a difference.

The tools we share with our CoMITs clients include our help desk ticketing system, our cloud-based documentation system, Microsoft Teams for exchanging files and ideas within a messaging system, network monitoring and our antivirus with EDR for all the servers and workstations (if applicable). With the use of Teams, we offer unlimited answers to

can work with you on other tools that you implemented internally.

There are many benefits to CoMITs, including:

- **Keep your IT person happy.** You love your IT person. Extra help means they can take that vacation or sick day without worrying about a call from the office. They work less overtime.

- **Cool Tools.** Your IT staff gets access to the same powerful IT automation and management tools we use to make them more efficient. These tools help us, and you, solve problems faster, improve communication, and make your IT far more effective and efficient. These tools are included in our CoMITs plan.

- **Pick our brains—there are many!** Got questions? Want another opinion? Ask! Regardless of whether it's covered or not, pick up the phone or utilize our shared Teams channel to start a discussion. We will help freely and openly.

- **Don't have time?** You can easily escalate a ticket/project/issue to us, and we will handle the issue for additional time and materials charges, at a discounted rate.

APs, routers, and firewall are also included here.

3.   Voice: This includes on-prem phone systems or hosted VoIP.

4.   Location: We can certainly segment work by location as well! For example, we handle sites A and B, you handle sites C and D.

Not only do we offer additional skill sets, but we also bring along our wealth of experience in proper management of IT. Our keys to success in CoMITs include:

Partnership

We believe a partnership is based on cooperation and trust. Your success is our success. Your goals will be our goals.

Openness

Transparency is king. All our cards will be on the table. All monitoring tools are shared with you, obviously different credentials and vice versa if you are bringing other tools in for monitoring.

Flexibility

We look forward to helping you implement strategic goals. What we cannot flex on are certain tools such as our ticketing system, documentation system, and RMM because those tools are tightly woven into how our company functions. However, we

relate to being that sole IT person in a big company trying to manage everything.

Co-managed IT is a broad term that encompasses any sort of ongoing partnership an internal IT team has with an external managed services provider (MSP). Our co-managed clients recognize that they have a wonderful IT person that needs some extra help or skills. In most situations, the internal IT person has welcomed us because they are exhausted from trying to learn all the new stuff on cyber-attacks and keep up with the day-to-day help desk issues. They can't really get a vacation because calls about IT problems and questions hound them no matter where they are.

How CoMITs are structured is open to interpretation, but my company offers these four areas of support:

1. Workstation support: Users need support for finding stuff (How do I open...?), training (I don't know how to use Teams...), printing (printer won't print/scan/power on), internet down (ugh!), and last but not least, help with line-of-business apps.

2. Server & infrastructure support: This includes both virtual and physical servers along with the *uninterruptible power supply* (UPS) that goes with them. Switches,

CHAPTER #6

CO-MANAGED IT (COMITS)

When I worked in the corporate world, I often had a third-party IT resource to help with special projects that I lacked experience in. I had no problem admitting what I didn't know so I could get my manager to bring in help. However, I was a voracious learner and would happily watch the senior techs at work so I could do it myself the next time around. Also, when I went on vacation, the third-party resources were on call instead of me for any IT problems that might arise. Today, managing an IT infrastructure is so much more complicated with all the cybersecurity threats. I can't imagine being in-house IT and not having external resources for help. IT is too big and too complicated for one person to keep up with and secure. That's why Next Century Technologies offers co-managed IT. I can totally

and vacation policy, disciplinary policy, theft, over-time definition, internet use policy, computer use policy, and any other policies specific to your industry. New employees should get a copy when hired and must sign a sheet confirming they have read it and are in agreement with it.

employees really like it. It helps me stand out in our local market. I also have a three percent matching simple IRA that I encourage all my staff to participate in.

We offer 15 days of paid time off. We also have a company car, so staff do not have to put a bunch of miles on their personal car (one pet peeve when I worked for other people!). I also provide a stipend every month to comp their cell phone bill because cell phones are required for their job. Extra benefits are much appreciated, and there are tons of ideas if you Google it. Keep in mind that your state labor laws will likely require that you offer all employees the same benefits. Refer to your HR expert before making changes.

Laptop

Buy your IT person a good quality laptop. Not a desktop, a laptop. Make sure it's a business-class one, or better yet, let the new hire pick one out. IT people must be mobile and work from anywhere in a pinch.

Employee Handbook

Do you have one? If not, write one or hire an HR agency to help. The Handbook helps you and your employees by spelling out the expectations of working at your company. The rules of the Handbook apply to everyone and should at least address work culture, flex time, tardiness, company vehicles, sick

Work culture

The attitudes of the people I work with mean a lot. I learned that lesson while I worked in the corporate world. So, I try very hard to keep toxicity out of my workplace. We have a small group (less than 10), so a little toxicity goes a long way. The older my candidates are, the more they understand that money isn't everything. We do a lot of employee luncheons and at least two events outside of the office every year that involve the entire family.

Bonuses

Who doesn't like to get extra recognition for a job well done? We have a bonus structure that includes realistic goals tailored to the job. Managers at my company meet monthly with staff to get feedback on how their jobs are going and to touch base on bonus goals. People want to be heard, and they want to be recognized for a job well done. If you don't have the money for a base salary, then put it in the bonus and tie performance to the bonus. Bonuses help build a positive work culture because it gives you an opportunity to shine the light on their hard work.

Benefits

If you can't really spend the money on bonuses or salary, then beef up the benefits. I provide 100% paid health insurance to each of my employees. Sounds steep and it is, but most companies don't offer it, and

process for us because only larger clients go to the trouble of trying to hire internally.

Right salary

You really get what you pay for here. But also, you can pay a lot and not get much in return. One of my most memorable projects was helping a beleaguered community bank following the financial crisis of 2009. The customer planned to fire their IT manager on a Friday at 5PM but needed to open the next morning at 9AM. My colleague and I had the job of securing a network of five bank locations, 18 servers, and 65 workstations that we knew nothing about in about 12 hours. Possible repercussions from a disgruntled IT manager were real, and we had to find all the back doors we could and change all the passwords. With the bank vice president's help, we secured everything by 3AM. But along the way, I found the IT manager's resume. It was stunning. He had been with the bank for over five years and had a litany of expensive Microsoft and Cisco certifications. It was way more impressive than my resume, yet I discovered the co-location that held all their servers didn't even have a properly implemented firewall. Lazy shortcuts were taken everywhere on the network, and I ended up doing a 10-page report on our findings for the bank.

passed. However, for most businesses, this is just not feasible. IT staff must be on-site every day. Here are some ideas that I have used to retain my talent:

Flexible hours

Can your IT person work from home one day a week? Can your IT person leave early to pick up a sick child from school? IT often includes nights and weekends—offering comp time or bonuses to reward this extra time at the office. Do note that offering such flexibility to IT might have to be applied company-wide. Check with the labor laws in your area.

Fair salary

I have seen companies hire candidates straight out of college because they can't afford the salary of someone with three years of experience. Well, they can afford it but don't want to upset existing folks who are paid less and do "more important work" and/or have seniority over this new hire. I get it, it's awkward, but that's the job market we are in. Candidates straight out of school are only qualified to manage the most basic networks. Depending on what degree they have, they may not be qualified to do anything but install Windows! Most of the time, they won't admit what they don't know and start making poor decisions on the network. When the IT person quits or gets fired, then we get called in to do the clean-up. This is usually a six- to twelve- month

they knew QuickBooks®. The first candidate was an older lady who was semi-retired and had years of QuickBooks experience. However, I found myself often helping her do basic functions within the program. Come to find out, it had been almost a decade since she had used the software, so I was basically having to pay her plus pay the agency fee plus spend hours of my time teaching her! I called the agency to tell them to not send her back and to send someone that they really tested, as their website promised. I'm happy to say the next candidate worked for me for many years, but after that, I was convinced that I could do a better job of hiring for less money. I committed to building my own hiring process. Headhunters may be a great starting point for you, but they don't know your IT infrastructure either, so they may struggle to find the right candidate. Be prepared to pay a hefty fee for this service.

Retaining the IT Talent You've Hired

Retaining talent when you can work from home for companies out of state is tough. Luckily, there are a lot of IT people that don't want to work from home for various reasons or they feel there is more to a job than money.

My company has chosen to do a hybrid work environment where we all come in a few days a week. We continue to do so even after the COVID threat has

The staff luncheon is always interesting. A few times, we've had a promising candidate get rejected by the rest of the staff. I learned quickly that our staff care about who they work with every day, so they are invested in the hiring process. Allowing them to have a say in the hiring process has been a win-win for both me and my staff. The quality of our hires has improved since I've implemented this one change.

If your company doesn't have a technical person to help write the IT job description or participate in the interview process, find one. You will waste considerable time and resources trying to find the right IT person if you do not have a technical background or are not familiar with the IT infrastructure in your building. Many of our bigger clients tried to hire internal first. More than one has told us how they had high turnover rates with IT people. Often, the quality of their hires was poor, and we spent considerable time fixing problems, replacing badly performing hardware, and documenting their IT infrastructure. If you don't have an IT resource to help, then I highly recommend hiring a managed service provider like me to manage your IT.

Let me take a moment to talk about headhunters or talent agencies. When I finally decided to hire a bookkeeper, I hired a temp-to-hire service just for accounting to help me get started. The website told me that they tested their candidates and guaranteed

- The second interview is over the phone by a technical person. It is followed up by an online technical test.
- The third interview is in-person at our office. It is usually followed by an invitation to lunch with the entire staff.
- We do a background check. This has weeded out candidates for us because even though we warn them there is a background check, some folks don't pass it!

Lots of spelling and grammatical mistakes on a resume is a red flag for us. It tells us that attention to detail is lacking and that writing is not important. For us, writing is critical—all timesheet entries end up on invoices, and we do a lot of documentation for the systems we manage.

The written questionnaire weeds out a lot of candidates as well. Our question is to explain the process of building a peanut butter sandwich. This is an opportunity to do some creative writing. And although there is technically no wrong answer, being able to write out the steps tells us this person can walk someone through a problem over the phone. You'd be surprised how many candidates don't respond to the questionnaire. That's OK; that's not a good candidate for us.

ble working in a team environment. This may or may not align with the personality you seek for your IT team. Sometimes, you want the best technical resource regardless of the personality package that comes with it. An IT person that appears to be aloof is not necessarily a problem unless this person is expected to work closely with others.

We have a written process for hiring. The basic elements of our hiring process include:

- A well-written job description with job responsibilities, clear expectations, and a notice that we require a background check.

- A resume review where we look for spelling and grammar mistakes, how often the person changes jobs, and does the work/education history line up with our needs.

- The first step is an emailed questionnaire to find out if they can write out a series of steps for solving a simple problem unrelated to IT.

- The first interview is over the phone by a nontechnical person to see how well they articulate. Do they answer in complete sentences and want to engage in conversation? Or is it quick, one-word answers to everything?

resources and leadership experience. He is a retired colonel and a graduate of the U.S. Army War College. He also worked in human resource departments while working in corporate America. He not only has faced many leadership challenges, but he has also dealt with labor laws at the federal and corporate level. Without his help, I sure would not have been as successful as I have been.

Hiring Talent

One of the hardest lessons I had to learn was to be quick to fire and slow to hire. I hate firing people, and it hasn't gotten any easier over the years. But every single time it turned out to be the right answer, and I have no regrets. Trust your instincts. Lack of performance, tardiness, and a poor attitude will spread throughout your department and help fuel a toxic environment.

IT people are, for the most part, introverts. We (and boy do I mean "we") struggle with interacting with humans. We can often be perceived as callous, uncaring, or egotistical because we are blunt and to the point. Small talk is not our thing. We also loathe to admit when we don't know the answer. My great challenge here is finding IT talent that is comfortable talking to strangers and patient enough to walk someone through a solution without sounding impatient or condescending. They also must be comforta-

you do? Banks fall under a variety of financial regulations. Does your IT vendor have experience with your financial regulations? Processes, procedures, and a critical eye for cybersecurity and accountability are a must for regulated industries.

☐ **They help you plan for growth.** Technology is an important part of your company's growth. Does your IT vendor help plan for events such as opening satellite offices, adding employees, building new locations, offering ideas on new applications to manage growth, etc.? Your IT vendor should plan, at minimum, a biannual technology assessment. They will help you design a technology roadmap for your existing and future growth and a budget to go with it.

Having Your Own In-House Staff

I own and run a managed service provider (MSP), but my challenges are the same as anyone else who is trying to maintain an in-house IT staff. My staff just so happens to provide help to other companies.

The greatest challenges I face are, first, hiring the right people, and second, retaining the right people. This was a huge challenge for me because computers, not humans, are my comfort zone. I was lucky in that my husband Joel has an incredible amount of human

HOW TO MANAGE IT IN YOUR BUSINESS

tion is a critical part of your business continuity plan; you can't do the plan without it. Get access to it if you don't already.

☐ **They help even when another vendor is involved or at fault.** Nothing is more frustrating than dealing with a technical vendor that blames you for their problems. We've all had the internet go down and the ISP (internet service provider) blames your router for the issue. The emails you send to just this one company are getting bounced, but that company blames your email service. You get told by the copier repair person that your copier's scan error is caused by your cabling, but you know it's not because it worked fine yesterday. We've all heard these lines before, and you just don't have the time or energy to play this game. Your IT vendor should be taking the lead on all these IT issues even if it involves an outside vendor. The goal is IT that just works, so make sure your IT vendor is making that happen, no matter who else is involved.

☐ **They have experience in YOUR regulated industry.** Medical industries and industries that handle patient data will fall under HIPAA requirements. Does your IT vendor know that they fall under HIPAA if

craft and maintain your business continuity plan.

☐ **They maintain documentation on your IT infrastructure.** Does your vendor have a list of all your critical logins and passwords? A diagram of your network that tells you what is connected and where? An inventory of all hardware sorted by age? A reputable IT vendor will document your network environment and keep it updated. A well-documented network can be managed easily by your IT vendor's team because important details are easy to find. An IT vendor with good documentation is a sign of stability and good stewardship of their clients' networks. Good documentation means that if an employee of your IT vendor leaves, someone else can easily take over!

☐ **They provide real-time access to your documentation.** Documentation is important if you ever decide to change IT vendors. Less scrupulous vendors will hold back documentation and passwords to make it more difficult for clients to leave. Ask for documentation. Better yet, ask for real-time access to it, which is easily provided by most cloud-based IT documentation solutions that your IT vendor can utilize. Good documenta-

hygiene. Certainly, your backups need to be secured offline." Your backups are the single most important remedy to an attack that will, not may, occur. Those backups must be reliable. So, did you get a successful backup report last night? Do they run at least seven days a week including holidays? When was the last time your IT vendor did a test restore? Ask!

☐ **They have a business continuity plan.** If data or hardware is lost or destroyed, are you covered? Can your business ride out any risk, be it a hardware failure, tornado, fire, busted water pipe, or ransomware attack? Do you have an alternate location if your building is damaged or destroyed? Can you function without the internet? Do your employees know your business continuity plan? How do you contact your clients during a disaster? Are there specific regulatory requirements for your industry, such as banking, that set mandatory recovery times?

If your business relies on technology, then your IT vendor plays a critical role in your business continuity plan. Employ an IT vendor that is not only well-rounded with technology but also skilled with helping you

cialized for one person to know everything. It takes a team to provide the skills, maintenance, and protection business technology requires. Not only will a team provide a better response time, but they will also have a diversified skill set for solving problems and building solutions. If your business relies heavily on technology, make sure you have an IT vendor that provides a team to manage it every day of the year regardless of sickness or vacations.

☐ **They have all backups tested regularly.** Frequent and successful backups are critical in a world of ransomware, hardware failure, and natural disasters. There has been a 70% increase in ransomware attacks in the past two years. CBS' *60 Minutes* ran a segment on ransomware on May 5, 2019, that every business owner should watch (https:// bit.ly/60ransom). In it, they explain how Ransomware-for-Rent websites allow anyone, regardless of experience, to run a ransomware campaign. Now, tens of thousands of ransomware emails and phishing attacks flood US-based businesses of all sizes every day. *60 Minutes* asked a security expert, "What is the best way to prevent this from happening?" The answer: "Great cyber

HOW TO MANAGE IT IN YOUR BUSINESS

right thing by law? A company that is not properly registered with the state is likely not carrying the proper liability coverage as well. This puts you and your company at risk if there is an accident. A "Certificate of Existence" from the Secretary of State may be relied on as conclusive evidence that a domestic corporation or domestic limited liability company is in existence. Ask your IT vendor for a copy of theirs, or search for one yourself online. Kentucky's Secretary of State website has a tool where you can do a business entity search. Look for a similar tool on your state government's website.

☐ **They have a record of longevity and experience.** With longevity comes stability. There are certainly great new companies out there, but it's difficult to understand their track record if they have been in business for only a short time. Weed out the fly-by-night folks by looking for vendors that have an established, positive track record. Companies that have been around a long time should have a list of references and testimonials.

☐ **They have adequate resources to solve problems in a timely manner.** Your technology is too complicated and too spe-

if it means replacing the hardware. Same goes for the services an IT vendor provides. People make mistakes. Does your vendor hold themselves accountable for their mistakes and resolve them quickly and without charging? If your IT vendor is not confident enough to guarantee their products and services, why should you be confident in your vendor?

☐ **They have proper business insurance.** You have car insurance and health insurance to cover yourself from the unexpected whether you're at fault or not. Your IT vendor should be taking the same precautions with liability coverage as well as error and omissions coverage. Make sure your current vendor is protected so that you are also protected. Request a certificate of coverage from your IT vendor. It's free and not an uncommon request.

☐ **They are registered with the Secretary of State.** Being a properly registered business (LLC, corporation, etc.) is a sign of commitment to both you and the law. It is a great step to ensuring they are complying with state laws, paying state taxes and workman's comp. Are they fully committed to providing quality service? Are they doing the

Outsourcing IT to a Managed Service Provider

If you have an existing MSP or are looking to hire one, here's a checklist of what the MSP should offer:

☐ **They give a guaranteed response time in writing.** It's important that you have a written agreement on how long it will take to respond to your issues. Having an SLA (Service Level Agreement), or guaranteed response time, keeps your IT vendor accountable to meeting the needs of your business. This is another method of reducing your downtime and giving you peace of mind that you know your issues will be resolved in a timely fashion.

☐ **They give a satisfaction guarantee.** It is important that a company stands behind everything they do and sell. If an IT vendor does not fully back the hardware or service they are selling, you could be left unsatisfied with the time and money invested in your technology. A "value added reseller" may be an old phrase from the 90's, but what it stands for is still important today—a hardware reseller who stands behind what they sell, and if you aren't happy with it, they should work diligently to make it right, even

your IT infrastructure. Computers that don't work cost us extra time and resources to fix, so our goals for technology align with yours—uptime and productivity. Not only will you make more money from your technology and staff due to better productivity, but we will be hyper-focused on protecting your network from risks such as ransomware, email *phishing* schemes, and hardware failure.

Another drawback I see with break/fix is that most often it's a one-person shop. That one person knows the most about your IT, and if that person is hit by a bus, their knowledge goes with them. They can get busy and not get back to you quickly. Sometimes they just disappear altogether (and companies like mine get a desperate call). They are often cheaper by the hour, but their cost comes into play when preventable problems are not dealt with and the server slows to a crawl, or someone clicks that phishing email and the mailbox gets compromised, or that seven-year-old computer running payroll fails.

In the next section, I will discuss the managed services provider (MSP) model. You will quickly see why I quit most of my break/fix work. It's much less stressful for me plus I enjoy building out an IT infrastructure that just runs well.

Forbes.com reported that over 75% of small-medium businesses suffered some sort of email compromise attempt in 2023, and that number is only getting bigger. Keep that in mind as you weigh the risk.

Now let's look at other scenarios in my list.

The IT Guy/Gal on Call

I call this the break/fix scenario. You break it, I come fix it. I did this for over a dozen years and still offer it to a select few clients. There's no ongoing management or monitoring of the IT environment. It can be a challenge because the IT person shows up and discovers that the environment has changed dramatically since the last visit. I don't like this type of work anymore because I was always two steps behind on what was happening, and what I saw happening was not good. Downtime increased because there was no preventative maintenance being performed.

What you need to know is that a "break/fix" IT vendor makes bank when you are down. Your bad situation works to their benefit. When you are down, you are losing money due to staff that can't work, plus you will be writing a big check to your IT vendor for every hour they spend fixing the computers. On the other hand, an MSP company like my own makes money when your computers are up and loses money when your computers are down. How this works is that we charge a fixed rate to maintain and support

from these types of home businesses. On the other hand, I was talking to a bank rep that had a client that owned a real estate title company. The owner has a half dozen computers, and he is also winging it. This type of scenario is much scarier. The title industry must abide by the Federal Trade Commission (FTC) security safeguard standards because they fall under the umbrella of financial institutions. The bank rep had mentioned that to the owner, but he was just clueless about it. I don't know much about the title industry. Perhaps they don't provide ongoing education for those companies. Educating companies like this is part of what we do. Hopefully, if we don't educate this company, the owner will take the time to educate himself.

If you fall under the "winging it" category, then you should really look at the risk to your company. If your company falls under a regulated industry, then you could face lawsuits and/or penalties for not following the standards when your company is breached. You may find it difficult to get cybersecurity insurance coverage if you do not have an experienced IT resource to help you meet the insurance company's requirements. Lying on an insurance questionnaire will only get your coverage denied if there is a breach. Your livelihood and your employees' livelihoods are at risk if you get sued due to losses others suffered by a breach of your network or emails.

CHAPTER #5

WHO IS GOING TO MANAGE YOUR IT?

Managing IT from a business perspective can be accomplished in one of several ways:
- You have a guy/gal you call when stuff is broken.
- You are outsourcing to an IT managed service provider (MSP).
- You have a staff in-house.
- You have in-house staff that partners with an MSP (Co-managed IT).
- You can wing it.

I had to add the last scenario to this list because I come across it quite often. I was at a business networking event yesterday afternoon. I often get asked what I do. One lady, after hearing my spiel, said, "Well, I just wing it." She was a travel agent working out of her home, so winging it is often what I hear

Remember!

Italicized words and phrases are found in the Glossary!

Sometimes, we have to replace equipment. Sometimes, the switches are just misconfigured, and once we straighten that out, it all runs well. Other times, the network has bottlenecks due to its design.

Summary

These are just some of the basic tools and techniques we use to manage all our clients. I did not really touch on cybersecurity in this chapter because although it is a critical part of IT, I have another book dedicated to it.

the desire to learn new things or that they never really liked keeping up and have kept the status quo for the past ten years.

How do you know if your IT person is letting their skills grow stale?

It can be hard to tell unless they have recent technical certifications. If most of the hardware around the office is over six years old and the server operating system has gone end-of-life, then these are signs that either money is tight or IT is coasting along. Most software vendors have some sort of training program that will provide a printable certificate. But for keeping up with the latest cybersecurity threats, it's not so easy.

If you have in-person IT staff, then make sure training them is part of your budget every year. A quality managed service provider will also require their staff to keep learning.

Network Performance

Another indication of good IT management is network performance. Are the computers slow? Do printers and Wi-Fi intermittently work? Is the network slower during certain parts of the day? If you have phones on the network, is the voice quality good? Outdated hardware, misconfigured hardware, and poor network design all impact performance.

a UPS because the local power company had regular drops and brownouts.

Surge protectors are the minimum for each workstation. We once had a client that had its own classroom of computers. Lightning hit. All but three computers were OK. The three that didn't make it were the ones without a surge protector. They work, and they are a cheap way to protect your investment.

Continuing Education

IT is the fastest changing industry in the world. We can't stop learning. Keeping up with IT is a huge part of my job. I am always on the lookout for new and better tools to manage and protect my and my clients' networks.

So how do I keep up?

I am part of several peer panels where I can talk to other IT professionals. I also subscribe to several newsletters and attend webinars. I like to read, so I don't gravitate towards video, but there's a bunch of content on YouTube. There's a ton of cybersecurity information on the federal government websites too, along with newsletters you can sign up for.

New technology and tools mean more classes and more learning. All of my tech job descriptions have the requirement of loving to learn new things. Regular online or in-person classes are expected. I've taken over clients from IT professionals that have lost

- Software and operating system updates.
- Alert monitoring, such as corrupt hard drives, services failure, low disk space, plus many others.
- Remote access to workstations.
- Age of workstations and server.
- Current status of workstations online/offline.
- Automation of tasks.
- Analytical reports.
- Network device discovery.
- Pushing out new software installations.

The software can offer a network map or at least provide the information needed for a network map. I like a map for organizations that have 10 or more computers at a single location. It should show the computers, switch, *firewall*, access points, and servers as well as the connections between them all. This is a critical part of IT documentation. As you can see, the right tools go a long way to improving IT management as well as improving security by keeping up with software and operating system updates.

Power Protection

All of the IT infrastructure needs a good power source, not just the file servers. We like to place UPS devices on all server and network equipment. However, I have seen several offices where each desktop had

portal, so people can submit their own tickets and track them. My ticket system is designed specifically for my industry, so the ticket entries go straight to a timesheet and an invoice. However, for internal IT, the timesheet part may be very appealing to management so they can track what techs are working on every day.

There are many ticket system options out there both in the cloud and self-hosted on your local server. The key to a successful ticket system, no matter the vendor, is getting staff to utilize it. This is where your policies and procedures come in requiring that all help desk requests are to be on a ticket.

Monitoring and Management

A good remote monitoring and management software tool is a worthwhile investment if IT must manage a lot of computers. We use ours for all sizes of clients, but a company looking to get one for their internal use needs to look at the monetary investment as well to see if it is worth it. Our monitoring and management software allows us to keep an eye on everyone's IT devices, no matter where they are located. Features include but are not limited to:

- Inventory of workstations and servers including hardware specs and software installed.

amazing how many different cloud products and vendors your company has when you sit down and audit them, and it's always interesting to see who has access to what.

For companies with file servers or cloud servers, an audit should cover who has access to which files and directories. The idea here is to give employees the minimum amount of access needed to do their jobs and document it. If there is a breach on that employee's login, this will give you a good idea of what data has been compromised. You will often find that ex-employees still have access to sensitive information. This is where that employee offboarding policy with a checklist can help prevent such mistakes.

Ticket System

IT personnel are always dealing with ongoing help desk issues. We manage issues through a ticket system. If you have an internal IT staff, I highly recommend a ticket system.

This will allow you to track who did what and when. It can also be helpful to identify if the IT department needs more human resources. Problems that reoccur may need a closer look to identify the underlying issue. Also, it can help techs solve problems quicker if they can refer to how a problem was solved in the past. Ticket systems come with a user

behind two-factor authentication, backed up by a solid, secure cloud-based vendor who is SOC2 certified. So, we use the password manager, Keeper®, and we encourage all our clients to use one as well. In fact, we are a Keeper reseller, and we only sell licenses with a how-to class. We find that more people will use it if they take a class and see just how much better their life is without having to keep up with all the passwords.

Business Continuity Plan and Disaster Recovery

We maintain this document in our IT Glue documentation management system. It provides basic steps to take to keep the company going in case of a disaster. You often think of weather events when you hear "disaster," but it really includes stuff like ransomware attacks and COVID.

Any event that can have a major impact on the company should be included. All companies should have a business continuity plan, and they should be checked annually in case they need updates.

Audit of Privileges

We do an audit of privileges at least once a year. So, my audit includes a chart of 30 different software and cloud platforms that we utilize plus those who have privileged (i.e., administrative) access to it. It's

Procedures that I have include the following:
- Onboarding of New Employees
- Offboarding of Employees (EVERY company should have one of these!)
- Privacy and Security Incident Procedures
- Daily Standard Operating Procedures
- Contingency Plan
- Business Continuity Plan and Disaster Recovery

Plus, hundreds more on such topics as answering the phone, responding to a compromised mailbox, human resource policies, and other topics related to the operations of my company and solving problems for clients. Having a well-organized documentation system such as IT Glue is key to keeping all of the above secure and easy to find for all my staff.

Password Management

We have a policy that all employees must use our password management system for company-related passwords. We actively discourage them from using it for personal passwords.

Why are we so picky?

We don't want passwords on sticky notes. We don't want passwords stored in browsers. We don't want passwords stored in Word or Excel documents. We want them stored in a secure online vault that is

that the company laptop is only for company business. It is not a toy to be shared with others in the household or to play games on. It is to be locked up safe every night. Desktops have their own policy as well. Both policies declare that the hardware is not to be used for illegal activities. Here are some of policies that I have in my organization. My company falls under HIPAA, so many of mine are mandated, but it's a good start for most companies:

- Desktop Use Policy
- Laptop Use Policy
- Internet Acceptable Use Policy
- Information Access Management Policy
- Computer and Information Security Policy
- Integrity Policy
- Device and Media Control Policy
- Password Management Policy
- Security Officer Policy
- Access Control Policy
- Security Awareness and Training Policy
- Employee Handbook (EVERY company should have one of these!)

action shot of the company's best IT guy in the city. Suddenly, he is hit by a bus. This leaves his teammates in a quandary of what to do now that his knowledge of their network has been lost. What is in the IT person's head should be part of a company's documentation system, either on paper or online securely stored where it can be accessed by the executives. That includes all the logins and passwords. The two-factor authentication codes should never go to a private cell phone. No logins for company-related vendors should be tied to private emails. This way, forgotten or lost passwords can always be reset with a company email. Never allow a third party to have complete control of your domain name. It is a very long and difficult process to regain control of a domain name from a third party that does not want to cooperate. No one wants to involve lawyers.

We manage all our documentation via a cloud-based product called IT Glue. We have it locked down in several ways to prevent unauthorized access. I recommend both two-factor authentication and IP locking for security. Your IT Pro can assist with setting that up.

Policies and Procedures

Policies provide rules, and procedures provide the how-tos. Do you have a policy on how employees are to use their company laptops? I do. My policy states

CHAPTER #4

WHAT DOES GOOD IT LOOK LIKE?

Whether you have a department of IT folks, a single IT person, or run an IT company, there are best practices that together provide a solid foundation for managing IT. Here are areas that I focus on in my IT company:

Documentation

After 30 years of managing computer networks for corporations and small-medium businesses, I have established standards of my own on what good IT stewardship looks like.

Some industries, such as medical and financial, have compliance standards they must adhere to. The one thing that I see that is sorely underutilized in IT is documentation, processes, and procedures. One of my favorite vendor commercials starts off with an

tion of only 30 days? That means if you accidently delete an email or folder, you have 30 days to figure it out and recover it. Retention rates vary by provider, and some providers offer nothing in terms of backup! If backups are not offered, is there a third-party product that can do the backup?

2FA

Two-factor authentication is critical to protecting your cloud data from ransomware. New ransomware attacks designed especially for cloud storage are becoming more common. Two-factor means you will need more than just a username and password to access your cloud storage account. You will also need a secondary method of identity verification, usually by means of a code sent to an email or smartphone. Is 2FA offered by your cloud provider? Set it up. If it's not offered, find a different provider.

Business Continuity

Catastrophes, like hurricanes and floods, can take out a data center, or at the very least, cut their access to the internet. Does your cloud provider actively replicate their data center to other sites around the country? Find out. A reputable provider will have this type of information on their website. It's a great selling point.

SOC2 Certification

Look for a cloud provider that is *SOC2 (Service Organization Control 2)* certified. SOC2 means a provider's information systems meets the standard for security, availability, processing integrity, confidentiality or privacy as set by the American Institute of Certified Public Accountants. Why? It means the provider is committed to security. These rigorous standards are added protection for your data. Financial and medical institutions look for providers that adhere to this standard. You should to!

Encryption

Is your data encrypted? Encrypted data is scrambled and requires a password key to unscramble. This keeps unauthorized people from accessing your data. Your data should be encrypted both in transit from your computer to the cloud and while it is stored in the cloud.

Backups

Your data is in the cloud, but that does not mean it is backed up! What if you accidentally delete a file? Is it hard to get back? What happens if ransomware hits your computer and the encryption spreads to your cloud storage? What if a disgruntled employee deletes all their files or emails before quitting? Don't assume your cloud provider is backing up your data—find out! Did you know Office365 has an email reten-

Google Drive, Apple iCloud plus many others. Just because it's in the cloud does not mean it is safe from ransomware, nor does it mean it's backed up! Microsoft recommends that Office365 users have a third-party product to back up their mailbox, Teams, SharePoint and OneDrive data. Always check the fine print or ask!

Not All Cloud Is Created Equal

My company protects and manages IT for clients from many different industries that use a wide variety of cloud-based applications. I have learned that not all cloud providers are created equal. "Free" is free for reason and comes with a price that is usually tied to poor security and your privacy or rather the loss of. If the service is free, then how is the provider making money off YOU? Chances are good they are taking a lot of shortcuts with protecting your data and selling your name and email to anyone willing to pay. If you need support, is there a support phone number, or do you email them and hope they respond soon? *If they disappear, what happens to your data?* All questions to ask if you are looking at cheap or free cloud storage.

When looking for a new cloud-based service for storing data including files, backups, and email, we follow the standards our bank clients must follow and look for these features in cloud storage providers:

CHAPTER #3

IT'S SAFE IN THE CLOUD, RIGHT?

Let's talk about what the "cloud" is for a moment, specifically as it relates to services found on the internet. The cloud is a computer or group of computers outside of your organization that provides services to you. Cloud resources are accessed over the internet, typically via a browser but could also be over a *virtual private network* (VPN).

I have had a few prospective clients tell me that they don't need cybersecurity because their data is in the cloud. This is just incorrect. Unless properly secured, hackers have the same access to your cloud application as you. If they can steal your login credentials, they have access to everything.

Hackers are creating malware and ransomware that run on your computer and target your cloud storage providers, such as Microsoft, Dropbox™,

phone, but Scott never lost another email or received a strange calendar appointment again.

Wipe your mobile devices before you sell or return them to the manufacturer. Ask your IT Pro or teenager to help you find the "reset to default" command. And pull those hard drives out of old servers and workstations too. Pay to have those drives shredded.

him a few test emails from different accounts, and they all came through. I changed the settings on his Outlook to check his email more often. (Back then, I had to manually set the sync rate.) I didn't hear from him for a few days, and then he called again. Emails were being deleted. I had to visit their office, so I told him to leave his laptop for me while he went on sales calls. At his office, I did some test emails between his laptop and my phone. Sure enough, about 30 seconds after my test email arrived in his inbox, it disappeared. Scott called in. He said someone had hacked his Outlook and put a doctor's appointment in Clay City on his calendar. Now, forcing someone to see a doctor in the rural town of Clay City, Kentucky, is hardly what I would consider modus operandi for a hacker! Suddenly, I had a hunch and quickly asked, "Scott, did you get a new phone?"

"Why yes, I did, and just last week sold my old one to a guy," he replied.

"Did you erase your contacts, calendar, and email off that phone before you sold it?" I asked.

"No...," he replied.

"I know what the problem is. The new owner is using your calendar and email because you left it configured on your phone."

I quickly hung up, and thanks to Microsoft, I was able to send a remote wipe to the phone. I wasn't certain what all the new owner is missing on that

business-class switches stored in racks to help protect them from the elements.

Firewalls have the same basic components as desktop computers. They will suffer in the heat and dust. They are usually kept in the same rack as the server, but I have seen a few on the floor under a desk. I like to plug them into a small UPS so if the power flickers, they do not lose connection.

Disposing of Hardware

I prefer to recycle all of my retired hardware. There are options that are free if you are willing to haul it and some that offer pickup services for a small fee. Check with your local facilities. However, before you dump that old server, desktop, or laptop, be sure to pull out the hard drive and have it shredded separately. That's a requirement for those companies that fall under just about any compliance, however, it's just smart for any business owner to do. I encourage you to take the time to do this extra step. A high school student that likes to tinker could be encouraged with soft drinks and pizza to pull the drives.

One of my absolute favorite work stories involves disposing of hardware. It's about a salesman for one of my clients. Scott had to be mobile, so he did a lot of work from his laptop and smartphone. Access to email was critical for his job. He called me one day complaining that his email wasn't working. So, I sent

All workstations (including laptops!) should be plugged into a good-quality surge protector. Beware that some fancy multi-port extension plugs don't have surge protection. Dollar stores, Walmart® and Big Lots® are some of the places you find these cheaper offerings. Study the label and make sure you see a joule rating on the label.

Joule is a measurement of how much power a surge protector can absorb. The higher the joule, the better the protection. Try to get one rated 1,000 joules for your workstation. I personally have had enough stuff zapped around my house that I have all my TVs, small appliances, refrigerator, garage door opener, and washing machine on quality surge protectors. When one stops working, the first thing I do is check if the surge protector burned itself out protecting my property.

Switches are more tolerant of the heat. Over the years, I have worked with several large manufacturers with massive metal buildings. I've seen manufacturing conditions so dusty that everyone was required to wear masks and another that was so damp that water collected inside the bottoms of the switch racks out on the factory floor. It's very difficult to control the temperature in these large buildings, which presents another challenge. Regardless, I have seen switches perform for many years in less-than-ideal environments. In every case, they were high-end,

ahead and replaced that unit, but that gave a whole new meaning to having a bug in the system!

Workstation Care

Desktops can also suffer from too much dust, especially if they sit on the floor. Desktops run fans that pull air through the system to cool it, which also acts like a vacuum catching all the dust, dirt, and pet hair on the floor.

Laptops rarely have dust problems because they usually sit up on a desk. However, the cooling vents can be blocked if the laptop is not on a perfectly flat surface. Also working outside in the sun can overheat a laptop if the temperatures are warm.

Extreme cold is a threat to laptops that are left in cars overnight. I always recommend bringing laptops inside due to the threat of car break-ins. Regardless, if temps dip below 20, I recommend bringing in the laptops. It's not good for the battery, and turning on a very cold laptop could damage the components.

Batteries in laptops are one of those components that don't last the life of the laptop. Every year, you get less runtime out of batteries. Newer battery technology has improved a lot over the years; however, I still like to run the battery down on my laptop (or phone) a few times a year. I feel like it extends the life of the battery.

temperature monitor that can be added. I don't like temps to get over 80 degrees. I keep a cheapo box fan at my office in case the air conditioning fails so I can aim that fan at the server. If that's not enough, I will shut down the server to prevent hardware damage. Early on, I rented second-floor office space from one of my clients. I had a rack of servers in my basement, and I was eager to get them out of the house. My basement was cool enough to keep them comfortable in the winter, but during the heat of summer, I had to run a fan on them 24/7. I thought my new office would be better, but we found that cooling the servers on the second floor of an older building was tricky, especially when the thermostat was on the first floor. There's a reason most server rooms are in basements or on the first floor.

One of my clients was a property management company that sat on the first floor of the condominium they managed. The IT closet was roomy, but unbeknownst to everyone was a big water pipe right above the server hidden by a drop ceiling. We all found out about it the day it burst all over the server below it. It pays to check what's sitting above your server.

If you have a dedicated server closet, check inside regularly. One of my team members discovered a client's UPS had been infested with ants. We went

drained the UPS battery and crashed the server. Then the UPS brought the server back up when power came back, resulting in many server crashes over a five-day period as the utility company cut and restored power while doing repairs in the city. Surprisingly, the server still booted, but even after six hours of Microsoft's help, I could only recover about 80% of the mailbox data in the Exchange Server. The rest was corrupted. To this day, I configure a UPS to shut itself off after it shuts down the server, or at the very least, configure the UPS to not bring the server up if power is restored. I also configure the UPS to notify me if there is a power issue so I can tell the client that the server and UPS have been shut down. That ice storm 20 years ago taught me an important lesson about the proper configuration of a UPS that I still follow today.

Location, Location, Location

Where you place your server is also important. A locked room with dedicated air conditioning is perfect, however, not always an option, especially if you are renting.

Please make sure your server area does not get too hot. In the past, I have added vents to doors and thermostat-controlled fans to keep the temps down. Keeping a thermometer next to the server is a great way to keep an eye on it. Some UPS units have a

In the last chapter, I talked about my vet clinic that had a disaster when the mirrored drives in their server failed one after the other in a matter of days. Since the scare that day at the vet clinic, I upgraded them to a Datto backup device that not only does the on-site and off-site backup, but it is also a computer that can take the place of a failed server using the backup that is stored on it. It's not as fast as the original server, but it gets the job done. Now that is a beautiful thing, as one of my law clients learned when they were hit by *ransomware*. A few years before, we helped their IT person replace all their servers and with them a new Datto backup device. The ransomware infected all their servers, but with our help, they recovered all the data from the Datto and did not pay any ransom. I get great satisfaction helping clients recover successfully from disasters, although I much prefer to prevent such disasters from happening in the first place.

For any server, it is wise to invest in a quality *UPS* with the appropriate load rating and run-time. The UPS should be configured to shut down the server automatically, and in every case, the UPS should shut itself down as well. Once, I was called to a new client to rescue a Microsoft Exchange Server after an ice storm kept the office closed for five days. The server was powered by a brand-new UPS that was never configured correctly, so repeated power failures

floor. I had pointed out the buildup of dust on the server's vents, but the client declined to let me clean out the server. Not long afterwards, that server failed spectacularly due to overheating. Multiple components were damaged. The 24/7 tow company was relegated to paperwork for a week while the server was repaired and the data recovered. Kudos to the office manager for having a business continuity plan in place for such a disaster. Heat and dust are issues for any computer or server. This same tow company suffered a lightning strike many years later. I had just installed a brand-new server and UPS. The new $400 UPS was toast, quite literally. Black ash spilled out of the back of it. However, their new $4,000 server was unharmed. Not taking a chance, I replaced the burned-out UPS with a quality surge protector until I could get the UPS replaced.

Don't forget, all servers need a good, reliable off-site and on-site backup. My company has a business continuity/disaster recovery product called Datto that tests our client backups every day. I sleep better knowing our backups are tested daily because I know what it's like to have a backup report successful and then when you need it, it fails. On-site backups are a must because they offer much faster restore times, which is critical if you need to be open the following morning at 8AM.

CHAPTER #2

HOW TO CARE FOR YOUR HARDWARE

The hardware that makes up your IT infrastructure is a significant asset in your company. Keep in mind that these devices often stay up and running 24/7/365. Simple maintenance steps will ensure that it lasts a long time.

Server Care

Even in a clean environment, every couple of years, check the air vents on the front and/or back for dust buildup. If it's extensive, it may need to be shut down and cleaned out.

I had a client that towed for the local police and had a large gravel lot. Their file server was on the second floor of a building that overlooked this lot. Even though the windows were never opened, staff brought in the lot dust on their shoes to the second

firewall hardware to the speed of the internet at your office. We recently added a new client that had an aging firewall and switch. They already had a nice fast internet connection, but everything was slow. Come to find out, the ten-year-old switch didn't support gigabit speeds. It was slower than the high-speed internet connection and thus dragging the entire network performance down. The old firewall couldn't go much faster than the old switch, which was another bottleneck. We replaced both devices.

All the computers saw an improvement in speed because their primary application was cloud-based, so fast network speed was important.

Firewalls

Firewalls are, at their heart, the border crossing between your company's internal network and the internet. Security subscriptions added to a firewall do provide better protection against hackers trying to sneak through the firewall gateway into your network.

The types of hackers and the different methods they use to get through are always changing, so a security subscription is necessary to keep up with the bad guys. Firewalls without a subscription aren't useless, however, they will not be good gatekeepers without the extra help. Most compliance regulations require the firewall to have an active security subscription. Many cyber insurance companies want to see it as well.

Firewalls are still popular today, but their roles continue to diminish as more and more companies are becoming "work-from-home" entities without an office building. For companies with workstations that are on the road or at home, security must be focused on the device itself or a cloud-based firewall through which all traffic passes.

Refer to your IT Pro for a business-class firewall, and do get the security subscription with it so that the firewall is regularly updated to protect you from the latest threats. Your IT Pro will also match your

most expensive switches at that time. I had my whole house on it, and everything worked. But my backups were hit and miss; I would get sporadic errors on their completion. I was buying a batch of new Cisco® switches for a client and added one for myself because my NETGEAR was around five years old. Well, wouldn't you know, ALL my backup issues went away when I installed that new switch. I didn't really notice any difference in how the other computers in the house were performing, but I learned then that switches can be sneaky. They don't just "die." Well, they can, but it's worse if they just start doing what mine had done—slowly failing. I like to age switches out at five years, sometimes earlier if there's a need for more speed or new features.

Don't make the same mistake I made. Buy the business-class switches. They will move data faster and have better quality components that are less likely to have issues. There are several switch manufacturers that provide a cloud-based or pc-based management platform that allows you to manage all the switches from one dashboard. We really prefer those types of switches because it makes configuration changes, backups, updates, and troubleshooting much easier. Refer to your IT Pro for a manufacturer that fits your needs and budget.

try. The hurricane that hits a Texas Amazon data center does not affect the Texas customers because the Texas VMs have been replicated to multiple other sites across the country. This is a very important feature if you are storing your critical company data in the cloud. Read more about cloud storage in Chapter Three of this book.

If you are considering virtualizing your servers, find an IT Pro that is certified in one of the major virtualization vendors. My company specializes in VMware, but there are several other big players out there. In fact, we offer virtualization projects to companies that have internal IT but not the experience to set it up. It's not a quick and easy skill to learn. Partner with a company like mine if virtualization is not in your IT person's wheelhouse.

Switches

When my company was in its infancy, I had a lot of servers to backup. I set up my own little data center in the basement of my house. The client backups would technically be off-site yet close enough that I could grab one and take it with me to do an on-site restore.

Internet speeds were much slower back then; a backup restore from the cloud would've taken days. I had what I would call a "prosumer" NETGEAR® switch at home, in other words, one of Best Buy's®

Virtualization

If you have servers in your office, then you need to know a little bit about *virtualization* and what it offers. I like to explain virtualization through analogy.

Virtualization has a physical host computer that is home to multiple *virtual machines* (VMs). These virtual machines can run any operating system, so they can be Windows/Linux servers or even Windows 10 desktop. Most often, they are servers, each of which has a specific function. Think of it like a fourplex apartment building. The outer shell of the building is the host, and each apartment is a VM. Hosts most often run on business-class server hardware and have a lot of disk space and a lot of memory. The disk space and memory are divided up among the virtual machines. A virtual machine is actually just one big file, so it's very easy to make copies of it for disaster recovery or for testing out new software or for business continuity if you keep a copy at a secondary site.

The other cool thing about virtualization is that if a VM runs out of disk space or needs more memory, it's very easy for the host to give it the extra resources it needs. It can even be automated. This is a very simplistic explanation of virtualization, but now think of it on a massive scale. Think Amazon or Google. Virtualization is how these giant tech companies can store the same data at multiple sites across the coun-

server was dying. The first drive in the mirror failed two days before, and we found the second failing the night before. The staff had no idea of how dire a situation they were facing. The bag full of chicken biscuits was for the staff because it was going to be an interesting morning. Their Dell server was only a year old, and I was expecting a replacement for the first drive failure to arrive soon. However, the flaw that caused the first drive to fail was also in its twin. My job that morning was to make sure the staff could work, albeit slowly, on the failing server while my team at the office restored from the backup to one of our own retired servers that I had kept around for training. Fortunately, the dying server continued to function, but I warned the staff to not enter any new data into it. The patient database on the server was only for reference. The failing drive could not be trusted. At 4PM, my senior engineer rolled in with our old server and brought it up as I shut down the dying server. The staff logged in and started entering all the updates to the patient files. The clinic did not miss one single appointment that day. No animals were turned away. I was very proud of my team that day! Once those new drives were installed, that Dell server performed flawlessly for over five years until it was retired.

- Last, but not least, find an IT Pro with server experience to set it all up correctly!

Backups are, of course, very important, and we will discuss more on that in the following chapter. However, I would like to mention drive mirroring. Often folks confuse drive mirroring with backups, but they are not the same thing. Mirroring, however, is an important part of a business continuity plan. Drive mirroring is when each drive in a server (or workstation) is copied to a second drive within the same machine. The second drive mirrors the first one, meaning data is written not once but twice. A server with mirrored drives can withstand the failure of one of the drives since the other has a current copy of all the data. We always sell servers with mirrored drives because drives can be a source of hardware failure. However, drive mirrors are NOT a replacement for a backup! You cannot go back in time to restore a file that was deleted yesterday. The drive mirror has no history you can turn to for a restore point.

Drive mirrors are not always perfect either. Mirrored drives perform best as a matched team. Sometimes this match can be a weakness. Back in 2018, I was standing outside the locked door of my veterinarian client at 7:20AM with a bunch of breakfast sandwiches in a bag and my laptop case hung over my shoulder. Trust me, it's never good to be surprised by your IT person before you open! Their

call queue for hours to talk to a nontechnical person who can only estimate when it will be back online.

I can't recommend memory or hard drive specs on a server without knowing more about its intended use. I defer to your IT Pro to help you select a server that meets your needs. Just remember, you get what you pay for when it comes to hardware!

Key points to making a server last six+ years:

- Buy more memory/disk/processor than what is needed today, or else you will find that in as little as two years, it won't be enough.
- Buy quality server hardware from a reputable manufacturer that sells business-class servers. Yes, you will pay more, but it will last longer.
- Buy a *UPS* that is smart enough to notify you when there's trouble and shut down the server. Poor power can damage server components.
- Keep the server and UPS in a clean, cool environment that is physically secure.
- Test the UPS every year, and replace batteries every two to four years.
- Keep the server operating system up to date.
- Keep users off the server console; password protect the console and lock it down.

Servers

I love servers. They are the foundation of my career, one of my specialties. The cloud has come along, and finally, with faster internet, makes most servers obsolete.

Before we recommend a server to a client, we always explore whether there is a better cloud alternative. But I still sell servers, and roughly half our clients still have them. Why buy servers and not go "cloud"? Lots of reasons. First, cloud is not a one-size-fits-all solution. It is simply another option to consider. Local servers provide:

- On-site performance that outperforms the cloud.
- Access to your data even if the internet goes down at the office.
- A less expensive option to cloud, most of the time.
- Control over updates and maintenance and associated downtime.
- Security: No third-party has access to your data (unless you give it or get hacked).

Most importantly, if your on-site server goes down, I can usually pinpoint the reason within 30 minutes. If you have a cloud application and it's down, you may not know why without waiting in a

ber right from the Dell website. Once you enter the service tag, a link to your computer's drivers and software downloads will appear along with build date and warranty status.

Bloatware

Most of the time, business-class desktops don't have all the extra junk software and games that come with consumer-grade products. Sometimes we must remove a trial version of antivirus, but most of the time, we can get the desktop shipped without it.

Recommendations for the Home

People often ask me what kind of computer to buy for home. If I can talk them into it, I recommend a business-class desktop or laptop. We have repaired a lot of cheap consumer-grade laptops. One new client had about 20 cheap 17" consumer-grade Inspiron laptops from Dell. Don't let the name fool you; I think maybe three of the 20 lasted three years. Cheap power ports and busted screen hinges doomed most of the units. A quality business-class laptop can cost a lot more than the ones at Best Buy or Costco, but they will stand up to more abuse. So, I always recommend that if you do buy a consumer-grade laptop, go ahead and buy the three-year warranty from the store. With just one claim, the warranty will pay for itself. And chances are pretty good you will need it.

easy to lose or steal. Windows Pro also nicely supports Microsoft Azure (now known as Entra). I defer to your favorite IT Pro to tell you the benefits of Azure/Entra when your office does not have its own file server.

Tool-Free Repairs

Dell's business-class desktops are made to be worked on with ease. The case can be opened up and all the major components can be swapped out without the need for any tools. All the release tabs for internal components are purple, making them easier to spot. It's rare that I swap out parts, but when I do, this feature makes my job easier!

Better Support

If there's an issue with a client's desktop, we will be the ones called in first to troubleshoot it. Before contacting Dell, we have a good idea of what part needs to be replaced. Dell support can be reached via phone, chat session, or email. We have found that chat sessions are easier than a call, and there's rarely a wait. Dell will ship replacement parts quickly, and most of the time, they will send a tech to install them as well. This minimizes downtime for the end user.

Warranty & Driver Availability

I'm not sure about other manufacturers, but Dell makes it easy to check the age and warranty status of any piece of Dell equipment via its service tag num-

several business-class lines that often (but not always!) come with three-year warranties, so they usually have better quality components. If it doesn't, I add it.

Performance

With better quality comes better performance options. A slow hard drive will bottleneck any system. Solid state hard drives are the standard now, thankfully. But you never know what you get with cheap consumer systems. I've seen them with slow, cheap "spinner" drives. Nothing drags a computer down like a slow hard drive. Sixteen gigabytes of memory is really the minimum to get nowadays. I start with an Intel® Core™ i5 processor but prefer the Intel i7 if the client can afford it. In business, fancy video cards are only needed for CAD (computer-aided design) systems or video editors or graphic designers. The extra heat and battery-draining effects of a fancy video card is usually not preferred in a laptop that does basic word processing, spreadsheets, and email.

Pro Operating System

Dell sells the Windows Professional operating system on its business-class computers. Why do I care? Pro includes BitLocker, a hard drive *encryption* software, that will make the contents of your hard drive unreadable unless the thief has your password. This is a must for laptop users because laptops are

My goal is to recommend servers that will meet their needs for six years and workstations for five years. Why the disparity in years? Quality server hardware will last six years, and the decline in performance is not as noticeable on a server as it is on a client's personal workstation. Why does it seem as though computers get slower as time goes on? The computers don't change, but the software that runs on them does. Operating systems have an endless number of updates and improvements. That slick new interface in Windows 10 was nice, but it demanded a lot more disk and memory resources to run. Windows 7 would happily run with eight gigabytes of memory, but now with Windows 11, we recommend twice that amount. Also, your endpoint security (AKA antivirus) software has a bigger appetite for resources as it's constantly being updated so it can watch out for new threats.

Workstations

When I quote desktops (or laptops) for a client, I always recommend business-class workstations for these reasons:

Quality

Most manufacturers, including Dell, HP, and Lenovo, make cheap, poor-quality computers, and you will get what you pay for. The big three also offer

CHAPTER #1

SELECTING THE RIGHT HARDWARE

The office manager at one of my clients called me wanting to replace her aging desktop with one from a local store that was on sale. I was not so enthusiastic because I knew those consumer-grade (i.e., for home use) desktops were not of great quality nor were they fast. I shared my concerns about it, but she pinned me down by asking, "But is it faster than what I have?" Well, of course, it was. Her current computer was over seven years old! That was all she needed to hear, and she ran out and got it. Two years later, it was replaced with a model of my choosing.

Why?

Because in two short years, the one she got was now too slow! Did she get her money's worth? I don't think so. The computer I recommended would've lasted over twice as long.

MANAGING IT IN YOUR BUSINESS

PART 2

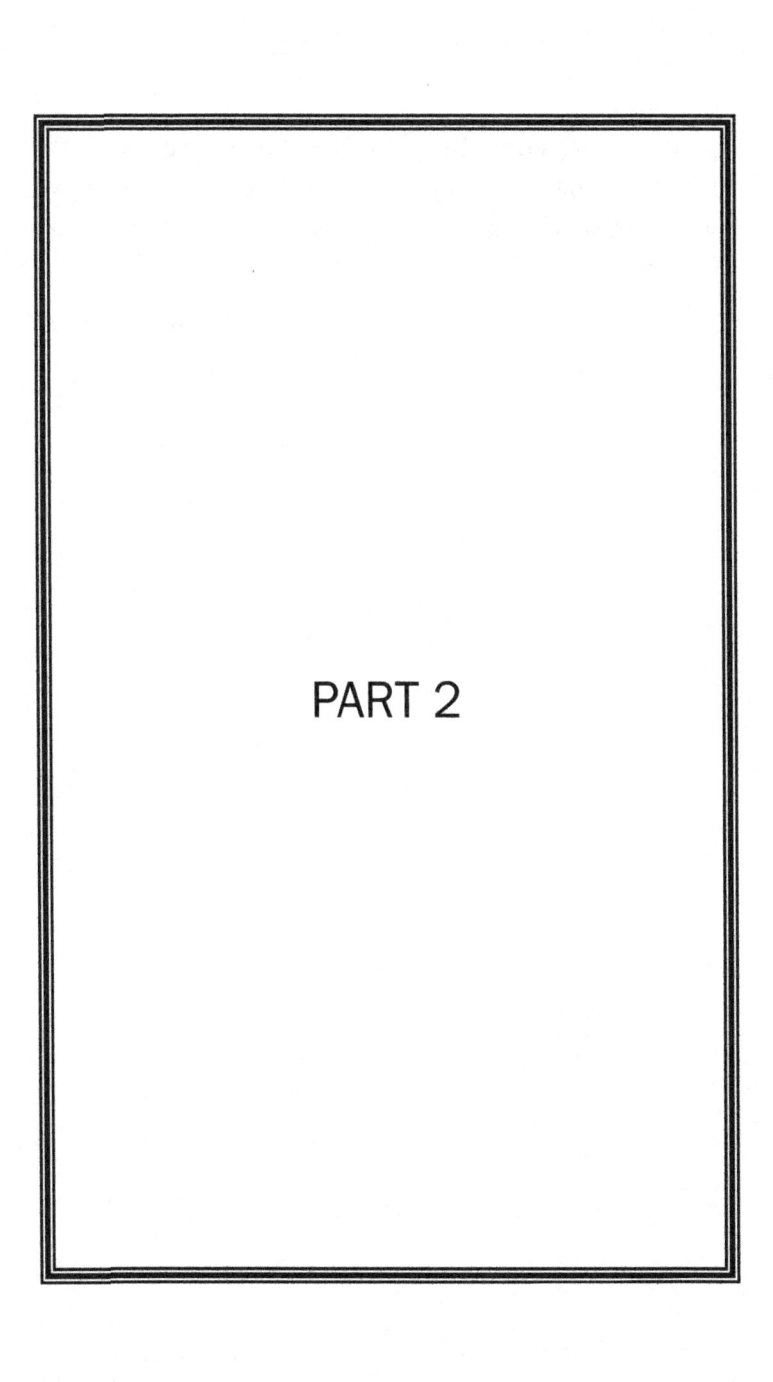

good introduction to what you can expect to face when finding help. And if you have, it's good to know what options are available in case you need to make a change.

—Tracy Hardin

old you-break-it-and-I-fix-it model. I didn't simply install antivirus and walk away; I installed antivirus and a management agent on every workstation and began proactively monitoring stuff. I didn't see a choice. Viruses and malware were becoming too sophisticated, and computers were being infected from just browsing the wrong website. I had to be more involved and needed better technical tools to properly protect my clients. In 2012, I had to hire my first employees to help with the workload as word-of-mouth referrals quickly outpaced my ability to keep up.

It's been 36 years since I got my first computer consulting job as a college student. Today, I see more and more of companies' budgets going to IT than ever before. I also see these companies make the same basic mistakes with their IT again and again. So, the first part of the book is more about operations and how the IT piece of the puzzle should fit into an organization. I will also discuss how to pick the right "*cloud*" and the right hardware for your business.

The last part of this book focuses on what good IT looks like. If you don't know the basics of IT management, how do you know if your IT Pro (either hired or in-house) is following best practices? Last, I write about finding the right IT Pro. I focus on three areas: (1) outsourced IT, (2) in-house IT, and (3) co-managed IT. If you have not hired IT help yet, it's a

going out on my own. Luckily, I was fired from that job right before Thanksgiving in 2000 for volunteering my IT skills at my church. While I didn't miss my old boss, I did miss the clients I was serving. I sent out Christmas cards to them with holiday wishes and that I would miss them. Soon, they all tracked me down via the return address on the envelope. These former clients became the foundation of what would become my foray into self-employment.

My new company, Woodford Computer Solutions (named for the county I lived in at the time), was started on January 1, 2001. I had a home office, a laptop, a bag of tools, and a pickup truck. My focus would be helping businesses with their computers. Back then, IT was a small enough world for me to be very effective at managing computer networks in all types of sectors, including insurance, TV/radio, construction, banking, medical, and various professional services.

A few years later, I moved to Lexington and changed the company name to Next Century Technologies, in honor of the new century we were in. My company grew by word-of-mouth; I did no advertising. By 2012, I had dozens of small business clients. The threat landscape had changed dramatically with *malware* rendering workstations and servers completely unusable. My business model became a "Managed Services Provider" (MSP) instead of the

computer labs as a consultant to help the students and faculty. There I got introduced to Novell NetWare, the most popular operating system at the time for personal computer networks. To earn my bachelor's degree, I did a lot of programming classes and quickly learned that was not for me. Managing personal computer networks with Novell was much more engaging.

I graduated from the University of Kentucky with a computer science degree in 1990. My years of experience as a student consultant at the University's various labs really helped because the nation was in a recession and jobs were scarce. I spent the next 10 years working in the corporate world. I worked for two government contractors, a third-party benefits management company, a large bank-holding company and finally with a small computer consulting firm here in Lexington. Along the way I got my Novell NetWare certification so I could build and design computer networks, which became the focus of my IT career.

Working for a computer consulting firm sparked a new love for me—helping businesses in all kinds of industries with IT. I really enjoyed seeing what goes on behind the scenes at these companies and how they leverage IT to improve their bottom line. I also learned a lot about how to not run a company while working for that consulting firm and considered just

INTRODUCTION

My name is Tracy Hardin. I am the president and founder of Next Century Technologies, an IT consulting firm located in Lexington, KY. I was introduced to computers in the early 1980's when my parents bought me my first computer, a Commodore VIC-20, for Christmas. I was interested in computers, so I took all the computer math courses that my high school offered. Since I found my computer classes to be easy, I picked computer science to be my college major. Luckily, it turned out to be a good choice because I had no idea of what else I wanted to do after high school.

In the late 80's, the University of Kentucky had several large computer mainframes which were used for research and for all my computer science courses. However, I really enjoyed working in the University's

online articles and videos, and you need to know them. So, if you see a technical term italicized, you know you can find out more about it in the Glossary of this book.

MY PROMISE TO YOU

I promise this book will help you improve your IT operations efficiency and perhaps give you a different perspective outside of IT being a high-dollar expense in your chart of accounts.

After reading this book, you will have better conversations with your IT Pro because you will ask better questions on IT maintenance and purchases. Or maybe you will take a second look at how computers slow down your day-to-day operations and have your IT Pro fix it. Maybe you are ready to find a new IT Pro because now you see where the one you have is failing you. Last, if you've been "winging-it" with IT, you may see the value in hiring an IT Pro after reading this book.

I don't shy away from all the technical terms because they are everywhere in the headlines of

So why am I writing a book? I'm a consultant; helping people is what I love to do.

WHO SHOULD READ THIS BOOK?

This book is written for those who are responsible for IT at their company. Depending on the size of the organization, this can be the CEO, COO, office manager or VP, sometimes even the CFO. These folks may have an IT Pro they can call, or they may have to fill that role along with their other duties. These basic concepts of IT operations apply to companies with either internal IT or outsourced IT or a combination of both (co-managed IT).

Are you the business owner that is "winging it" when it comes to IT? Plowing along and fixing your staff computers as problems pop up, or do you have an employee that's pretty good with IT? Now may be the time to up your game. This book will show you how to do that or help you find the right fit if it's time to outsource your IT.

Tracy is an invaluable resource for practical business IT knowledge, as demonstrated in this book. It is an excellent read for anyone thrust into an IT role as part of their primary job duties. Tracy excels at demystifying our industry's jargon, making the information accessible to everyone.

I first connected with Tracy Hardin on various business IT forums. She later founded the IT Documentation Users Group (ITDUG) on Facebook (fb.com/groups/ITDUG), and I joined her in managing it. Over time, I've had the pleasure of spending time with Tracy, her family, and her team at Next Century Technologies at numerous IT trade shows.

If you are looking to support stellar individuals who will, in turn, enhance your business through superior IT services, this book is a must-read. Consider partnering with a company like Next Century Technologies for your IT needs.

—Allen Edwards

Author of *Process and the Other 'P' Word*
(Which Is Also Process)
My businesses past and present: HiQ Networking, HiQ Internet, Eureka Process, MSP Hire, Trickster's Hideout, EPI Consulting, Gozynta

FOREWORD

As an author, speaker, entrepreneur, and IT industry expert, I was thrilled when Tracy asked me to write the Foreword for this book. Owning four businesses, I understand the value of outsourcing IT needs to proficient teams like those at Tracy's Next Century Technology. Focusing on revenue generation and leadership is crucial; I can't fathom managing IT infrastructure without insights like the ones shared in this book.

IT infrastructure is essential for maintaining competitiveness in today's market. Whether you handle IT tasks yourself or outsource them, the knowledge within these pages will equip you with the basics needed to effectively communicate with IT professionals, ensuring your infrastructure robustly supports your business operations.

WELCOME

PART 1

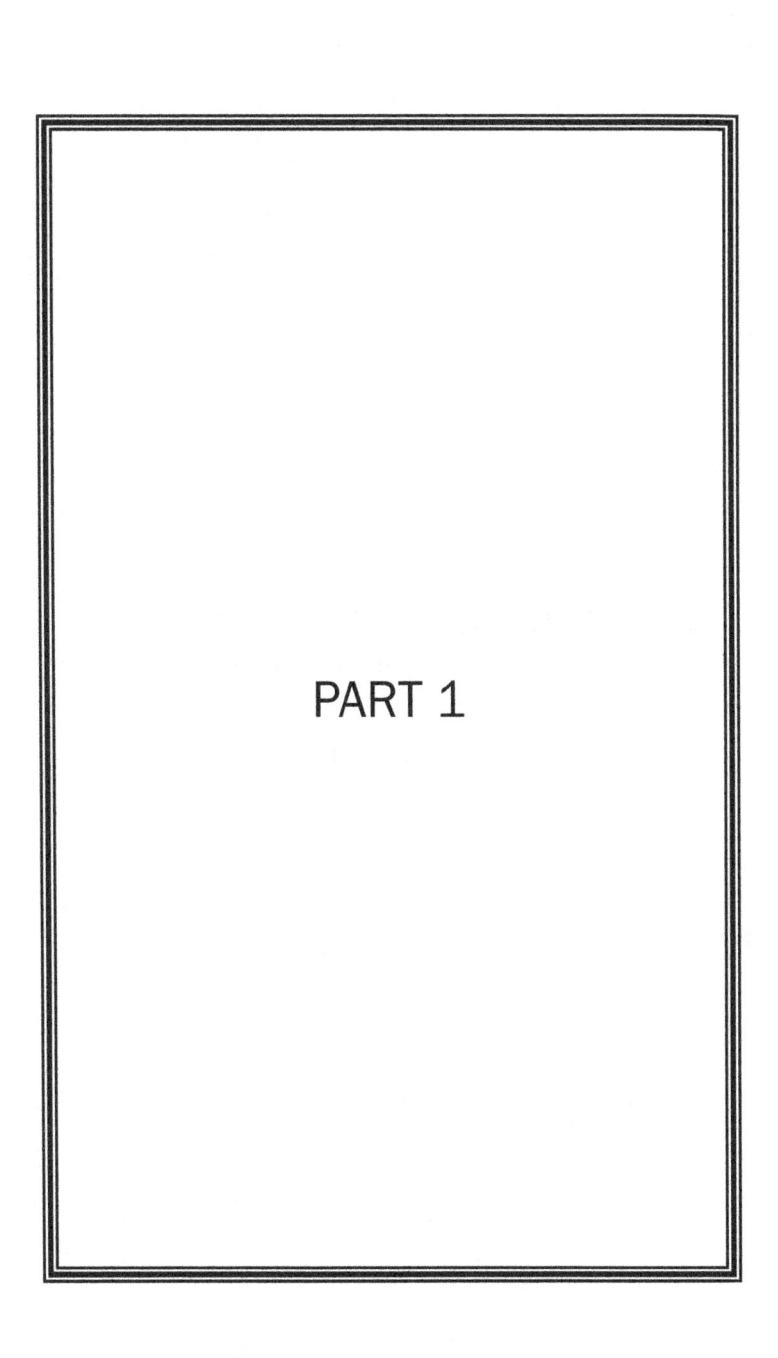

I dedicate this book to my husband, Joel Hardin. Without his help, I would not be the successful business owner I am today.
I love you.

CONTENTS

Part 1—Welcome
Foreword 1
Who Should Read This Book? 3
My Promise to You 5
Introduction 7

Part 2—Managing IT In Your Business
Selecting the Right Hardware 15
How to Care for Your Hardware 29
It's Safe in the Cloud, Right? 39
What Does Good IT Look Like? 43
Who Is Going to Manage Your IT? 55
Co-Managed IT (CoMITs) 77

Part 3—The Path Forward
Who Relies on Us? 87
ProCare Managed Services
by Next Century Technologies 91
The Next Step 97
About Tracy Hardin 99
A Small Request 101

Part 4—Glossary
Glossary 105

PUBLISHED BY NEXT CENTURY TECHNOLOGIES

Copyright © 2024

All rights reserved. Without limiting the rights under copyright reserved above, no part of this book may be reproduced, stored or introduced into a retrieval system, or transmitted, in any form or by any means (electronic, mechanical, photocopying, recording or otherwise), without the prior written permission of both the copyright owner and the publisher.

052024

DISCLAIMER:

While all attempts have been made to verify information provided in this publication, neither the author nor the publisher assumes any responsibility for errors, omissions or contradictory interpretation of the subject matter herein. This publication is designed to provide accurate and authoritative information with regards to the subject matter covered. However, it is sold with the understanding that the author and the publisher are not engaged in rendering legal, accounting, or other professional advice. If professional advice or other expert assistance is required, the services of a competent professional should be sought. The purchaser or reader of this publication assumes responsibility for the use of these materials and information. Adherence to all applicable laws and regulations, including federal, state and local governing professional licensing, business practices, advertising and any other aspects of doing business is the sole responsibility of the purchaser or reader.

**What You Need to Know About IT
Without the Geek-Speak**

HOW TO MANAGE IT IN YOUR BUSINESS

A Guide to Demystifying IT Operations
for Small and Medium Businesses

TRACY HARDIN

Also by Tracy Hardin:

*How to Cyber Secure Your Business:
A Guide to Demystifying IT Security for
Small and Medium Businesses*

FREE BONUS CHAPTER

Unlock the secrets to avoiding costly IT blunders with an exclusive bonus chapter, "**The Top 10 Mistakes Business Owners Make With IT.**"

Don't let your business fall victim to security breaches, inefficient processes, or outdated technologies. This bonus chapter reveals the most common pitfalls companies face when managing IT and how to avoid them.

From implementing scalable solutions to leveraging innovative tech for a competitive edge, this free download is a must-have for anyone serious about mastering information technology management.

Don't miss these pivotal lessons, which are available exclusively to our readers. Visit our website now to download your free copy and turn IT challenges into opportunities!

Sign up here: https://NextCenturyTech.com/chapter

Or scan here: